MULTICULTURAL FOUNDATIONS OF
PSYCHOLOGY AND COUNSELING

Series Editors: Allen E. Ivey and Derald Wing Sue

Multicultural Encounters: Case Narratives from a Counseling Practice
Stephen Murphy-Shigematsu

To Sean

重松

Stephen

Multicultural Encounters

Case Narratives from a Counseling Practice

Stephen Murphy-Shigematsu

Teachers College, Columbia University
New York and London

Published by Teachers College Press, 1234 Amsterdam Avenue, New York, NY 10027

Library of Congress Cataloging-in-Publication Data

Murphy-Shigematsu, Stephen
    Multicultural encounters : case narratives from a counseling practice /
Stephen Murphy-Shigematsu.
        p. cm. — (Multicultural foundations of psychology and counseling)
    Includes bibliographical references and index.
    ISBN 0-8077-4259-7 (alk. cloth) — ISBN 0-8077-4258-9 (pbk. : alk. paper)
    1. Cross-cultural counseling   2. Cross-cultural counseling—Case studies.   I. Title.
II. Series.

    BF637.C6 M86 2002
    158'.3—dc21   2002071972

ISBN 0-8077-4258-9 (paper)
ISBN 0-8077-4259-7 (cloth)

Printed on acid-free paper
Manufactured in the United States of America

09   08   07   06   05   04   03   02   8   7   6   5   4   3   2   1

Contents

Series Foreword

Counselors and other mental health professionals are increasingly encountering clients who differ from them in terms of race, culture, and ethnicity. Unfortunately, most clinicians have been trained in psychological models derived primarily from a Euro American worldview. As a result, few are culturally competent—that is, prepared to understand how culture affects the definitions of normality and abnormality, as well as manifestations of mental disorders, and awareness of the need to balance culture-universal and culture-specific approaches in treating a diverse population.

Multicultural Encounters: Case Narratives from a Counseling Practice transports the readers into the inner world of the client, taking us on a multicultural journey where issues of race, culture, and ethnicity are revealed as dynamic and powerful dimensions of human existence. Stephen Murphy-Shigematsu does a superb job in bringing to life the hopes, fears, conflicts and aspirations of people through their life stories—stories that illustrate the importance of culture. His comprehensive narratives allow us to view the human condition holistically: Clients possess individual, group, and universal identities that are inseparable. His insightful analysis forces us to understand why Euro American atomistic approaches that analyze clients into thinking, feeling, or behaving beings are too limited and fail to recognize that we are all of these and more. He reminds us throughout that we are also social, political, spiritual, and cultural beings.

When first published in 1955, Robert Lindner's historic book *The Fifty-Minute Hour* mesmerized professionals and the lay public alike with its description of the inner workings of traditional therapy. While fascinating and influential, its monocultural focus was a disservice to the clinical field because it served to perpetuate the notion that culture was unimportant in therapy. This bias was largely invisible to readers, since the profession at that time lacked a multicultural lens by which to view the clinical encounter. Murphy-Shigematsu's book is truly revolutionary and brings a more complex, comprehensive narrative to the therapeutic table. In his book, we learn to recognize the delicate balance that characterizes individually and culturally sensitive therapy. The author is among the first to present clinical acumen in multicultural narrative form, thus enriching our understanding of client dynamics and the human condition. This book serves as a valuable treasure trove of stories that professionals and students can use to understand multicultural thought and through that understanding to enhance their practice.

The constant theme throughout these therapeutic narratives is that meaningful work with clients must consider each unique individual in his or her social and cultural context. Murphy-Shigematsu's book brings us fascinating narratives of people within cultural systems; as their narratives unfold, so does the complexity of their interrelationships and interactions. It is not just race and ethnicity but also important sociodemographic markers, like class and gender, that define culturally sensitive counseling and therapy.

As co-editors of the new series from Teacher College Press on the *Multicultural Foundations of Psychology and Counseling*, we are delighted to present Stephen Murphy-Shigematsu's book. We consider it one of the truly foundational contributions to the practice of multicultural counseling and therapy. This is not just a book to be read and studied, but also one to enjoy.

Allen E. Ivey, Distinguished University Professor (Emeritus)
University of Massachusetts, Amherst

Derald Wing Sue, Professor
Teachers College, Columbia University

Acknowledgments

To my family, who nourished and sustained me and whose love is written on these pages.

To the mentors who guided, inspired, and believed in me.

To the persons who shared their stories.

To the friends who encouraged me.

To those who supported and worked directly on the book.

To all a deep thanks and appreciation.

Multicultural Encounters

Case Narratives from a Counseling Practice

CHAPTER 1

Prologue

So healing is the receiving and full understanding of the story so that strangers can recognize in the eyes of their host their own unique way that leads them to the present and suggests the direction in which to go.
(Nouwen, 1966, p. 68)

One day when I was a student in graduate school, the professor asked the class to discuss whether there was enough culture and race in our counseling psychology curriculum. To my surprise, several classmates claimed that since we had a cross-racial counseling course, there was sufficient attention given to these issues. I countered that, other than the minorities, few students took this course, and voiced my feeling that issues of culture and race needed to be integrated into every class. The discussion solidified my position as an advocate of the centrality of cultural concerns in counseling and my ardent pursuit of clinical training, education, and research in this area.

Over the years I have heard numerous grievances from persons dissatisfied with their counselors' inability to understand them. This impotence was sometimes attributed to the counselor's race, but usually to a lack of awareness of and sensitivity to the person's cultural background and an absence of curiosity and openness to exploring it. Being viewed through the cultural lens of such a counselor, they felt "defective," "deficient," "underdeveloped," or otherwise labeled simply for their racial appearance, values, or ways of being to which they had been socialized. The counselors, they claimed, were not even aware that they were looking through a cultural lens, but simply assumed that everyone saw the world as they did. These reports have encouraged me to continue to make culture an integral part of the education of mental health professionals.

However, I have often felt discouraged by the effects of my efforts. One problem became clear to me as I was relating the story of a Korean woman who was troubled by her relationship with a manipulative mother, and her dream that revealed the underlying tension between them. The story

1

was fascinating to me, so I was surprised to notice that some students seemed frustrated and restless. Finally one complained, "But that kind of problem is not just Korean!" And of course she was right. Not only Koreans have problems with their mothers. In every society there are mothers and daughters and probably issues of control that are revealed in dreams. But what intrigued and disturbed me about the student's comment was her apparent assumption that the story of a Korean woman should somehow be "Korean" from start to finish, and her disappointment and puzzlement to find that in some ways it was a common human drama.

As I reflected on the class, I realized that I had faced a similar situation myself when I went through years of specialized training in providing psychological services for American ethnic minorities in the 1980s. Despite my enthusiasm for participating in the vanguard of what we anticipated was a growing movement in the field of mental health, I often felt disappointed by the training. In retrospect, I think that my disenchantment was partly because I was always looking for the cultural aspects and ignored the human motivations. I felt that if the story of an ethnic minority client had universal or individual themes not related to culture, it somehow detracted from the specialized nature of the blossoming field. It was some time before I realized that such an exclusive focus on culture was distracting me from attending to the uniqueness of the person in front of me in the counseling room and the absorbing existential themes in their lives.

My training in multicultural psychology preceded the current state of heightened awareness of the importance of considering culture in assessment and therapy. The attempts of academics and clinicians to dismiss culture and discover universal knowledge about human psychology have been discredited (Mio & Awakuni, 1999). Psychology can no longer pretend to be neutral and anything more than a way of knowing practiced in certain places at a particular point in history (Sampson, 1993). There is a growing acceptance of the cultural assumptions of normal and abnormal development, psychological processes, illness, and therapeutic intervention. Advocacy for mental health rights of various minorities has highlighted the great danger of the exercise of power in the helping professions (Ponterotto & Casas, 1991). More professionals are willing to believe that the mental health field has been guilty of ignoring, stereotyping, and pathologizing certain segments of the population (Pierce, 1970). Some will admit that institutionalized cultural bias has led to underserved minorities and inattention to culture in clinical situations, research, and counselor education (La Fromboise & Foster, 1989). There is greater understanding that biases of counselors cause suffering and that counseling is an instrument of oppression when certain cultural values are transmitted implicitly or explicitly to our clients (Sue & Sue, 1990).

The flourishing diversity of the American population has also made it impossible for clinicians to ignore the demands presented by their increasingly multicultural clientele. Yet few mental health professionals have received education and training regarding cultural considerations in clinical work and may be stuck in a culturally encapsulated way of relating with their clients. Simply out of necessity, more clinicians are searching for an understanding of how to integrate culture into their practice.

But what kinds of education and training are suitable? The most widely endorsed multicultural counseling competencies define three basic areas:

1. counselors' awareness of their own assumptions, values, and biases;
2. understanding the worldview of the culturally different client; and
3. developing appropriate intervention strategies and techniques (Sue et al., 1998)

The prominent method of teaching has been to provide cultural knowledge of specific groups. Much of the literature has emphasized the education of the White counselor through acquaintance with the minimal necessary knowledge to work with African Americans, Asian Americans, Latinos, and Native Americans. This approach outlines the group's history of immigration, acculturation, and discrimination as well as general cultural characteristics and recommendations for assessment, counseling, and therapy when working with a member of the group. More reductionist writing ignores social factors and paints a description of minorities as having exotic, culture-bound disorders and a set of cultural traits.

ETHNIC NARRATIVES

In these circumstances, the idea that there is a fixed, invariant, and essential Black identity that can be held constant while supposedly superficial differences like money, power, and sex proliferate is a defeat. . . . In its strongest form, this type of essentialism represents the wholesale substitution of therapy for political agency.

(Gilroy, 1995, pp. 16–17)

The discourses on ethnic minorities that have thrust the field of multicultural counseling from the margins onto center stage have inherent limitations. The problem is that it is extremely difficult to teach about something that is supposedly specific to a whole group without generalizing. Although we know that we are not supposed to essentialize, we find it hard to talk about groups without doing so. So we acknowledge the diversity that exists within groups, declare affinity with postmodernism, decry essentializing, and then—unsure of what else to do—proceed to generalize.

A specific ethnic group is constructed by emphasizing homogeneity, unity, and timelessness and by disregarding differences, smoothing over contradictions, and minimizing conflicts and movement. A particular culture is described in terms of an enduring set of characteristics, behavioral traits, or beliefs, which members of that ethnic group are expected to share. These descriptions lead the reader to conceive of what is inside the constructed boundary as a discrete entity with fixed traits. The result is an unwitting contribution to the invention of essentially peculiar ethnic others who can be separated from an essential self (Abu-Lughod, 1991).

Despite their antiessentialist intent, the new images offer no escape because they are based on the same concepts of race and culture that tend to freeze differences (Said, 1978). Well-meaning but illusory absolutes ironically share the similar quality of ignoring culture's relentless evolutions and metamorpheses, making cultural stereotypes and alternative representations two sides of the same coin (Chow, 1993). Oriental/Occidental, Black/White, Asian/White, or other dichotomies fix differences between "us" and "them" in ways so rigid that they may be considered innate, incarcerating Others in time and place (Appadurai, 1988).

Reductionistic writing that emphasizes a narrow view of culture fails to recognize migration and ethnicity as fundamentally social, not merely cultural. It therefore denies the ways in which laws, ideologies, and popular beliefs about nationality and race influence a person's experience (Good, 1998). Viewing ethnicity simply through cultural characteristics also distorts the ways in which minorities are oppressed by economic and educational processes and exaggerates the homogeneity and stability of cultures by denying differences based on sex and class (Dyson, 1995).

While this kind of writing encourages counselors to consider culture, the danger of such writing is that it freezes culture in time and space. Expectations we develop from such material can distort our sense of the wholeness of the persons who come before us, turning the minority client into an object rather than a person. The focus on cultural differences ignores certain aspects of human experience and by feeding prejudices can become an insurmountable barrier to empathic understanding and communication.

The language of generalization and the distancing discourses of psychology cannot convey the nature of the people we write about. Case histories written in professional, scientific language fail to communicate the complexity, passion, and pain of the emotional dilemmas faced by individual human beings. Since I first began the study of psychology, I have hungered for a form of writing that allows us entry into the intimacies of individual lives. Each individual who comes before us lives not as an "African American" or "Asian American" programmed with "cultural" or "racial" traits, but as a human being going through life agonizing over decisions, suffering injuries, struggling with isolation, trying to find meaning, enduring losses, achieving insights, confronting mortality, and finding moments of happiness. That all of these experiences are deeply influenced by culture and race does not make them any less human. If we lose sight of this we are lost as counselors. When we see someone more as Black (or White) than as a human being, our connection is dangerously warped (Vontress, 1979).

By presenting individual stories in this book, I am suggesting that the demands on counselors go beyond the acquisition of culture-specific, generalized group knowledge, and must include the complexities of cultural borderlands and multiple levels of cultural realities in a person's life. We who work with clients from diverse backgrounds are challenged to cultivate a respectful curiosity and openness that allows us to look beyond our assumptions and stereotypes to learn from the client. Multicultural counseling is considered a consciousness that guides all counseling, rather than a set of skills and generalized knowledge.

Comprising narratives from the therapy process that emphasize both the client's healing and the counselor's development, this book tells the stories of five persons who come from a variety of cultural backgrounds, all clients with whom I have worked. Although the cultural backgrounds of the clients may be unfamiliar to some readers, I believe that the stories presented here have relevance to the field of mental health in general. They are the stories of people of different cultures; they are also human and existential stories of unique individuals.

Although clinical psychology and psychiatry have a long tradition of emphasizing the presentation of individual cases, it is only from the 1980s that psychological processes have been reinterpreted in light of recent writings about narrative (Bruner, 1990; Sarbin, 1986; Spence, 1984). This view focuses on how human experience is organized, remembered, and transformed through stories people tell about their lives. Humans give meaning to their lives in narrative terms by seeing themselves as living in the drama of particular stories.

In this book I present an approach that experiments with narrative clinical ethnographies to complement existing discourses of multicultural counseling. These are individual stories and cultural generalizations are avoided. Showing the actual circumstances and detailed history of individuals and their relationships suggests that such particulars are always present and crucial to the experience of any individual. Such narratives depict both human similarity and variability within groups and across groups as well as previously unarticulated experiences of borderlands. This approach celebrates the unity to be found in a diversity of individual narratives rather than searching for grand unifying narratives in a system of similarities (Hayes, 1994).

AN INTEGRATIVE MULTICULTURAL COUNSELING FRAMEWORK

Counseling and therapy's effectiveness is enhanced when the counselor uses techniques, strategies, and goals consistent with the life experiences and cultural values of the client.

(Sue, 1995, p. 654)

The therapy presented in this book is grounded in an integrative framework of multicultural counseling and therapy developed by Derald Wing Sue and colleagues (Sue, Ivey, & Pedersen, 1996). This is a metatheoretical approach that recognizes that all helping methods exist within a cultural context and represent different worldviews. Conventional counseling is regarded as just one approach among multiple helping roles developed by culturally different groups around the world.

Person-Centered and Culture-Centered

Operating within the structure of conventional counseling, this multicultural approach emphasizes that our effectiveness is enhanced when we set goals and use methods that are congruent with the life experience and cultural values of the client. Responding to a particular client's needs may include modifying the kind of relationship that we offer. Working with individuals from more traditional cultures who expect greater authority in a counselor challenges us to recognize the limitations on individual freedom imposed by a person's culture and society, while maintaining liberation as expanding consciousness of self in relation to others as a basic goal of counseling.

While this approach is person-centered, it is also culture-centered in the sense of recognizing that reality is based not on absolute truth but on understanding complex and dynamic relationships in a cultural context. A culture-centered approach views the client's situation as formed and embedded in multiple levels of experiences and contexts with every person having three basic aspects: He or she is like all others, like some others, and like no others (Allport, 1962). A simultaneously integrated perspective is called for, and ignoring or overemphasizing any of these aspects is likely to be harmful to the counseling relationship.

Exaggerating cultural differences results in a stereotyped, exclusionary, politicized, and contentious perspective. On the other hand, focusing on cultural similarities can lead to the exploitation of less powerful groups, the denial of diversity, a pretense of homogeneity, and dismissal of ethnic identity (Ivey, Ivey, & Simek-Morgan, 1997). Seeing only the idiosyncratic denies the importance of person in context and human similarities. Attention to this totality and interrelationship of experiences and contexts is regarded as a fundamental of counseling.

Our cultures are viewed as developing from the experiences we have and also from the stories that we learn in our socialization into different groups. Cultural-identity development is stressed as a major concern that deeply affects the client's, but also the counselor's, attitudes toward the self and toward others of various groups. Each client is believed to have multiple cultural identities and selves and counseling emphasizes the development of the self in relation to and connection with others. While accepting that development may occur in stages, its varied, cyclical, nonlinear, nonhierarchical qualities are also recognized (Katz, 1999; Parham, 1989). The various levels of identity are therefore fluid and ever changing so that the salience of one aspect over the other is always in flux. In counseling, the focus on individual, group, or existential issues constantly shifts, requiring us to struggle with validating these different levels and sensitively relating to that which is most salient to the person at that moment (Ivey, 1995).

Mainstream and Alternative

The counseling presented in this book integrates various traditions and schools of psychotherapy, both mainstream and alternative. Training in traditional East Asian medicine preceded my socialization as a psychologist and informs my understanding of illness and healing. This training, with its emphasis on holism, unity of body and mind, and person-environment fit, instills a concern with the mental health effects of a client's mundane daily activities such as eating, drinking, sleeping, and exercising (Kaptchuk, 1983). Principles of cultivating discipline and feelings of gratitude, respect for elders and ancestors, humility, and acceptance of self and fate are meaningful in the clinical context. Although these principles vary in their applicability to persons of different cultural backgrounds, the conception of the individual as intimately connected to a world beyond the self, embedded in family, community, and a spiritual world, guides my attempts to work with all clients (Murphy-Shigematsu, 1999, 2001a, 2001b).

Related forms of largely nonverbal indigenous Japanese therapies teach the importance of other types of communication besides the word, and other modes of healing (Morita, 1998). The discipline of meditation teaches us how change is as dependent on how we are able to simply be with ourselves as with what we do to try to improve ourselves (Kabat-Zinn, 1995). Therapies that employ a nonverbal mode of intervention remind us of the significance of our messages in counseling that are transmitted without words (Reynolds, 1982). One of the great limits of stories is that as a verbal medium they cannot convey well the unspoken intimations and connections that occur in our encounters.

Humanism and Existentialism

Another major theoretical influence here comes from humanism, as a philosophy of human equality and a deep tradition of caring, of respect for individual choice, and of the importance of relationship (Rogers, 1961). The depth of the simple principle of active, nonjudgmental listening is repeatedly brought home to me as I attempt to provide human company for my clients (Morimoto, 1972). Trying to understand the world as my clients see it, to empathize with their pain and struggles, involves mutual learning and liberation (Taft, 1973). Attention to the importance of assuming responsibility for our own construction of the world, for choice, and for acting intentionally is continually stressed in these stories.

Much of the distress of people is viewed as flowing from the individual's confrontation with the givens of existence and ultimate concerns of their own isolation, the imminence of death, and the meaning of life. This existential framework emphasizes the instinctual feeling and sensing of the counselor rather than a manual approach. This involves carefully shifting attention to vital concerns of the client and our responses to them, and making them central rather than peripheral to the therapy (Yalom, 1980). In this tradition, the infinitely various life experiences, including pain, suffering, and turmoil are regarded as opportunities for growth (May, 1969). The attention to ultimate concerns also includes a focus on the spiritual life of the individual (Vontress, 1996).

Constructivism and Narrative

The third area of theoretical influence prominent in these stories is a constructivist narrative therapy approach. This philosophical context respects clients as active agents who individually and collectively co-constitute the meaning of their experiential world (Neimeyer, 1995). Reality may therefore be invented, and also situated in a context (Efran & Clarfield, 1996). This consciousness that the belief systems and apparent realities are socially constructed rather than given, and hence can be constituted very differently in various cultures, is especially important in multicultural situations. The liberating view of problems as problems, rather than persons as problems, works against our professional desire to classify, diagnose, and label and the biases we exhibit in these acts (White & Epston, 1990). This view guards against the tendency in individual therapies to emphasize responsibility for the problem in the client, failing to see how fault can also lie in the environment and therefore blaming the victim (Sue, 1995).

The nature of the counseling in this book is further guided by an emphasis on interpreting the linguistic and discursive means by which people construct their selves. The structure of human lives is viewed as inherently narrative in form, in which people constitute and are constituted by the stories that we live and the stories that we tell (Spence, 1984). Because counseling is sought when our stories become ineffective, it involves the editing of old restrictive stories and the composing of new liberating stories (Gergen & Kaye, 1996). Attention is also placed on the reflexivity of counselors in viewing the explication and reconstruction of their own therapeutic stories over the course of therapy.

Weaknesses, Excesses, and Balance

Although each of these traditions is instructive, they all have their own particular weaknesses and excesses. Traditional therapies are often criticized as maintainers of the status quo, by their lack of attention to social change and personal liberation (De Vos, 1982). Their philosophies and goals usually seem to be simply to help the person adjust to the society rather than to encourage individual or environmental change. The focus on gratitude, respect for those in positions of authority, and acceptance of fate can lead to self-defeating, passive forms of resignation to an oppressive structure.

Humanism is discredited in poststructural and postmodern circles as a philosophy that has continually masked the persistence of systematic social differences by appealing to an allegedly universal individual as hero and autonomous subject (Clifford, 1980). It is attacked for its failure to see that its essential human has culturally and socially specific characteristics that exclude most humans. The refusal to see how we as subjects are constructed in discourses related to power limits the usefulness of humanism.

The postmodern approaches are also criticized as exaggerated and utilitarian (Held, 1995). Is truth simply what works for you? The claim that there are multiple realities can mean that no one can say that one way is better than another. The rejection of all attempts to posit essentials and universals can be extreme in its nihilism when declaring that nothing is real and nothing is authentic. Emphasis on the story can become a denial of experience, and an overemphasis on spoken words is inappropriate for individuals from certain cultural backgrounds. Assertions that reality is constructed can lead to denial that there are also essential facts of experience (Schwarz, 1998).

The integration of these and other theories in clinical practice is often problematic. Paradoxes and contradictions abound as we attempt to embrace certain principles while accepting their limitations. The concept of intentionality can be useful as a key existential construct that holds that people can be forward-moving and can act on the world, yet must remain keenly aware that the world acts on them as well (Ivey et al., 1997). We could also envision a "tactical humanism" in which we are liberated by a sense of infinite possibility that is balanced with an awareness of cultural limitations (Abu-Lughod, 1991).

An integrative approach attempts a harmony of alternative, indigenous, and mainstream therapeutic traditions, modified by a consciousness of the centrality of culture and a philosophical context of social constructivism. Integration of different schools of therapy could also be described as striving for balance in which various perspectives are regarded as valuable contributions to our understanding. Balance means that understanding and reconciling discordant opposites and tolerating inconsistency and dissonance are vital capacities for the counselor to cultivate (Pedersen, 1997).

We are challenged to maintain balance in many ways:

- Respect for individual satisfaction and free choice with an appreciation of the individual as embedded in family and society.
- Belief in the necessity of assumption of personal responsibility for present actions and therapeutic change with knowledge of the blame that can be attributed to others for one's problems.
- Emphasis on verbal expression with an understanding of the nonverbal intuitive, indirect manner of communication.
- Appreciation of the value of contemplation with acknowledgement of the need for action.
- Attention to differences with focus on commonalties.
- Utilization of cultural identity and other stage theories of development with a cognizance of the fluid, unpredictable, uncategorizable nature of a life story.
- Respect for the scientific methods of psychology with an awareness of the artistic nature of counseling and the mystical nature of our spiritual connections.

COUNSELING AS ART AND NARRATIVE

Indeed, the capacity to tolerate uncertainty is a prerequisite for the profession. Though the public may believe that therapists guide patients systematically and sure-handedly through predictable stages of therapy to a foreknown goal, such is rarely the case. Instead . . . therapists frequently wobble, improvise, and grope for direction. The powerful temptation to achieve certainty through embracing an ideological school and a tight therapeutic system is treacherous: such belief may block the uncertain and spontaneous encounter necessary for effective therapy.

(Yalom, 1989, p. 13)

Although approaches to counseling that outline clear stages and strategies are expanding the possibilities of psychotherapy as a science, they still fail to account for the artistic factor in what we do. There is an undefined quality of therapy that limits our ability to describe exactly what happens and what heals. Resisting the allure of becoming a follower of an orthodox method of doing therapy means attempting to respond to the individuality of each client and accepting the ultimate uncertainty of what occurs in the therapeutic situation.

I am reminded of a woman in Japan who prepares delicious natural food for troubled guests who come from near and far for her therapeutic meals. She never uses a recipe but tunes in to the essence of the vegetables, which she has grown herself, and senses just how much each needs of various spices and preparations to acquire their ultimate taste. Each individual piece of vegetable or fruit she touches is different and therefore each product is also unique and not reproducible with a cookbook.

Similarly, counselors are challenged to attempt to tune in to the essence of the person, both like and unlike any other person who has sat with them before. We can try to tolerate the anxiety of not knowing, the feelings of helplessness, and the impulse to withdraw from the client's experience (Shainberg, 1983). Together with the client we may attempt to engage in a struggle to discover an insight, a moment of awareness, trusting in our sensitivity and intuition to introduce what will enhance our understanding. Without a manual there are no predetermined steps and interventions to follow but all depends on the particular person's state at that precise moment. Diagnosis may consist of a constant checking of where a particular client is in a particular moment, and therapy of our attempts to relate with them in each moment. A sensitive therapist relates differently with different clients, and with the same client at different times (Kahn, 1997).

This book paints personal portraits of some existential human dramas of struggles with freedom, isolation, and meaning. Humans are seen as the authors of their lives, capable of handling the awesome responsibility of structuring their own reality. Therapeutic interventions described here aim at freeing individuals to generate new ways of thinking, feeling, and acting, transforming personal mythologies that guide their actions and choices (Parry & Doan, 1994). The goal of therapy is therefore more creative and exploratory than corrective and directive, as it attempts to foster the broader development of a client rather than alter cognitive distortions (Neimeyer, 1993). Interventions are reflective and intensely personal rather than persuasive, analytical, and technically instructive. Focus is on present understandings in the service of future actions rather than on past actions in the service of present understandings (Hayes & Oppenheim, 1997).

Counseling is viewed as a narrative practice in which people tell stories about themselves and their experiences and the counselor listens and tries to help them tell their stories more deeply and fully (Goncalves, 1995). We attempt to enable people to confront and recall previously hidden stories of shame and pain. When a client repeats his or her story without any apparent benefit, the goal of therapy is to deconstruct and rework the narrative so that the client learns new ways of valuing the past, understanding how it has led to the present, and imagining the future. The story that emerges must be convincing and compelling and allow new meanings and options. As we build a more therapeutic narrative together, we engage in a battle of liberation from the problem.

The reconstruction of the old narrative may involve enabling clients to recognize themselves as victims of particular forms of injustice or oppression by interpreting the stories we hear from them as political stories, stories of abuse, or human rights violations. The task of the therapist is then to discourage resignation as a passive victim of circumstances and to encourage the individual to take control of the stories that master his or her life. They may then become able to retell their stories in ways that transform their memories and reshape their lives. Culture determines what is an effective or therapeutic story, one that will promote healing and enable one to recover. The recognition of the metaphoric structure of psychological experience and the strategic use of metaphors in psychotherapy are thus complex cultural processes (Good, 1998).

Whatever their background, counselors can help develop culturally appropriate healing stories by cultivating the curiosity to learn and remain attentive to the meanings expressed in the client's narrative. Clients may be approached from a position of "not knowing," of trying not to fit them into cultural stereotypes, and instead to learn from them (Anderson & Goolishian, 1996). General and theoretical knowledge of clinical processes and cultural patterns of behavior may guide us but is secondary to knowledge of the individual.

Counselors also can tell stories that help clients to make sense of their lives (Omer, 1998). These may be related to culturally appropriate and powerful myths or master narratives that make sense of human weakness, actions, and suffering (Harter, 1995). Or we may employ strategic metaphors that attempt to reduce distance from emotions such as rage or humiliation and allow the person to gain access to the feelings he or she denies when asked directly about them. We may help clients to see how they are caught in a web of largely unconscious metaphors and to escape and create new ones.

Since we are listening for the unique and fascinating stories in each person's life, counseling can be seen as closely linked to the artistic and imaginative process of storytelling. In this sense, it is very much a creative act. Jung (1965) asserted that he was intentionally unsystematic, because therapy with individuals demands individual understanding and a different language for every patient. Yalom (1989) carries this concept even further by suggesting that if we take seriously the notion of uniqueness, we need to invent a new therapy for each client.

THE REFLEXIVE COUNSELOR

As a doctor I constantly have to ask myself what kind of message the patient is bringing me. What does he mean to me? . . . The doctor is effective only when he himself is affected. "Only the wounded physician heals." But when the doctor wears his personality like a coat of armor, he has no effect. . . . Perhaps I am confronted with a problem just as much as they. It often happens that the patient is exactly the right plaster for the doctor's sore spot. Because this is so, difficult situations can arise for the doctor too—or rather, especially for the doctor.

(Jung, 1965, p. 134)

Therapy is viewed as a heroic and very personal quest, both for the individual and for the therapist, who is simultaneously engaged in the process. Understanding and accepting our own experiences and biases that assist and impede us in seeing others more clearly is therefore regarded as an integral part of therapy. Self-awareness is a source of empathic experiencing and our greatest aid in escaping the inevitable limitations in understanding others. Obvious gender, ethnic, class, or national differences are only extreme forms of other, less apparent, cultural differences between client and counselor. As we recognize these differences and begin to close the gaps—discovering new ways of seeing and being together—the stories of client and counselor come together with each life course altered by the experience (Howard, 1991).

Therapy is regarded as a relationship that is as much about who the therapist is in relation to the client as who the client is in relation to the therapist. The stories therefore emphasize therapists' self-narratives, the way we define our identity and ourselves as persons. Counselors also bring their own worldviews to the relationship and these affect the way they conduct therapy. Therapy therefore involves the counselor working through and developing self-understanding about problems that arise from his or her own self-narrative as reflection-in-action (Schon, 1984).

The focus on the counselor's thoughts and feelings may seem excessive or self-indulgent to some readers. Despite my occasional embarrassment at self-revelations and fear of a descent into a careless use of reflexivity, I have risked this approach because I believe it captures the essence of the experience for counselors, who can understand the nature of our own experience far better than they can know the client's. Although we may long for deeper communication with our clients, our awareness is usually stuck on the level of our individual consciousness. During therapy we have moments of connection, perhaps even experience a healing aura, but mostly we are struggling with our own thoughts and feelings and this is what I try to capture in this book.

A focus on the counselor is also chosen to reveal the self-learning that can take place. I hope to illustrate the belief that counselors who are able to explore, understand, and accept themselves are better able to confront a diversity of situations. The counselor is challenged to remain an objective observer who can provide guidance, while also entering into a relationship in which he or she is affected and changed by the encounter. But by engaging with the client the counselor is exposed to the same existential issues as his or her clients and so must be prepared to examine them.

In the stories in this book I was confronted with a variety of demands. Could I help a woman of an outcaste background to develop a positive identity when my own empowerment was based in pride in my elite samurai ancestors? I wondered how I could help an effeminate, emotionally fragile mixed-ancestry youth confront discrimination when my own narrative of overcoming racism was so macho and stoic. I struggled to not turn away from the anger and paranoia of an Iranian man, when I find these so frightening in myself and others. A young Korean Japanese woman challenged me to help her understand her issues of identity while I was trying to distance myself from my own extended identity conflicts.

These cases offer a view of the therapist as a reflexive being who regards the review and reconstruction of his or her own therapeutic stories over the course of treatment in the same terms as the narrative revisions made by clients. The therapeutic encounters here reflect a constructivist position that the therapist is not acting as a blank screen but is engaged in a co-constructive process where the therapist's hopes, fears, and life experiences play an important role in shaping the unfolding of the client's life story. The therapist attempts to face the anxiety and use the reality created between himself or herself and clients in his or her own life (Leitner, 1995). The challenge is seen as the negotiation, renegotiation, construction, and co-construction of viable and sustainable ways of being for both the individual and the therapist.

No matter how well we prepare ourselves professionally, the encounter with another human being seeking relief from suffering invariably challenges us in unexpected ways. The therapeutic encounter, like any intimate relationship, is full of mystery, surprise, and unpredictable twists and turns. If we are honest, we must admit that we are often unsure and at a loss about how to be helpful. When we perceive this situation as a threat to our sense of expertise, we may see it as a sign of failure or defeat. But if we can accept these moments of uncertainty, they can be opportunities for opening to occur (Katz, 1999). They challenge us to let go of our mental agenda, put aside our cherished theories and beliefs for a moment, and pay closer attention to the person with us, forcing us into a more direct relationship.

Accepting our helplessness and vulnerability forces us to slow down, become more attentive, and wait—which allows space for creative possibilities and a larger intelligence in us to take over (Welwood, 1983a). The most effective healing occurs when we drop the attachment to being the expert and open ourselves to the client (Morimoto, 1999). We often resist this call because we are threatened by the fears and anxieties of the client that too closely mirror those unresolved areas in our own life (Yalom, 1980). Yet one hopes that the connection with the client keeps opening our heart despite our attempts to pull back and assume a more distant, safe, and professional position (Katz, 1999).

Opening to a client's situation allows a counselor a chance to work on these issues in one's own life. Struggling with one's own resistances to this kind of engagement with a client reveals new awareness and wonder in counseling. I have often been grateful to clients for waking me up from my numb, half-asleep, preoccupied state of being through sharing the genuineness of their painful searching. Without losing my boundaries, the more I can let myself experience what the other person's reality feels like the better I am able to respond from a place of true empathy and compassion (Welwood, 1983a).

WRITING STORIES OF COUNSELING AND DEVELOPMENT

My aim is not to make a system, or to see patients as systems, but to picture a world, a variety of worlds—the landscapes of being in which these patients reside.

(Sacks, 1990, p. xviii)

The stories presented in this book started out as unilateral in nature, reflecting my views of the client's reality. However, I realized that I was treating myself as an expert, while denying this expertise to the client. I then requested and included the clients' observations in the research process. In this way both of us gave something to and gained something from the evaluation process (Viney, 1988). Respectful inquiry is research *with* rather than research *on*; clients become persons who are partners in the research process, rather than objects of study.

These stories are not meant to be representative of multicultural counseling. My experience is limited and in no way represents this vast field. The narratives represent only the lives of these individuals and our attempts at healing. The stories of others would be unique and would include different conflicts, different cultural backgrounds, and different paths of healing. Multicultural counseling in other settings would include more work with families, children, assessment, interpreters, indigenous healers, and other variations.

The stories in this book represent my attempt to understand the intimate encounters I have had through counseling and to share what I have learned from years of working with individuals of diverse cultural backgrounds. The cases presented come from my clinical work in the United States in San Francisco and Boston, and in Okinawa and Tokyo in Japan. I believe they have relevance for multicultural practitioners in many countries. Although this introduction is written in a traditional academic style, what follows is quite different. My guiding principle is to never write anything that the educated layperson (or I myself) would not understand. I have purposefully avoided jargon that may be incomprehensible to readers and that unnecessarily confuses and creates distance.

These are true stories, but to protect the privacy of clients certain changes have been made. In the writing process, some forgotten moments were retrieved and dialogue was reconstructed through reflection on clinical notes and comments of these now-former clients. In the end, what emerged are stories in which, like all history, "fact" and "fiction" are no longer clear.

During the writing of this book I came across these inspirational words attributed to Jesus in the Gnostic Gospels: "If you bring forth what is within you, what you bring forth will save you. If you do not bring forth what is within you, what you do not bring forth will destroy you." These words helped me to recognize our work as something to be shared, thereby overcoming an uneasiness with the self-centered, egotistic arrogance of presuming that writing about one's experiences and reflections would be of value to others.

The concern that one must know more before writing a book was relieved by words from Fijian healers that the "straight path" is silent and humble work in which one keeps to the truth, saying only what one knows, "no more and no less" (Katz, 1999). This is what I try to do in my counseling and teaching, and in my daily life, and adopting a different voice in my writing would be false and inappropriate. Therefore, in this book, I have tried to tell only what I know: no more, no less. But it has not been an easy challenge. The temptation to want to tell more than I know in an attempt to earn the respect and admiration of readers has been there throughout my writing. I hope that I have not succumbed to this seduction too often.

My hope in writing this book is that those who read it will be better able to provide help to those they meet—assisting friends, colleagues, and clients to be free in whatever responsible way the person chooses. While we are all under cultural constraints, we are also endowed with the ultimate freedom of controlling our own minds and therefore our own reality. It is my hope that counselors can have some positive influence on this freedom in the persons we encounter.

CHAPTER 2

The Boy Without a Song

I celebrate myself, and sing myself.

(Whitman, 1983, p. 22)

An aura descends on us like a mystical shroud that envelops and unites. There is a gentle but powerful emanation and radiance. Perceptions are sharpened and the realization hits that we are truly together. The distance between us evaporates and the room is filled with an energy that illuminates it. Sense of time and space is altered and there is only the present moment.

I rhapsodized about such fleeting and rare encounters as my mind wandered. Of course, this doesn't happen every day. And nothing like that was happening that day. I longed for such a connection in my work with Hideo, but with him therapy was painfully slow and uneventful. From the beginning he spoke little, and answered questions sparingly. Our afternoon meetings dragged on in the hot and humid Okinawan summer. It had been a long time since rain had fallen and water was now being rationed. I prayed for a break in the clouds, and wondered when relief was in sight, for the parched land as well as for our dreary sessions.

I was in Okinawa conducting a research study on the experiences of the children fathered by Americans with local women. More than 50 years after the end of World War II, tens of thousands of American military men still populate the main island of the southernmost prefecture of Japan. Some fathers take their kids to the United States, a few fathers remain in Okinawa, and many others simply leave the children behind—children locals refer to as "the kids left by the bases." In Okinawa thousands of mixed-ancestry Amerasian offspring live around the sprawling military bases, negotiating the complex political and racial dynamics of their communities.

One day I received a phone call from a young man. He had heard that I was a counselor, he said, and wondered if I would see him. Since I still had to arrange for office space, we agreed to meet in a coffee shop in town. After I hung up the phone, I realized that we hadn't bothered to describe the way we look. Rather than this being an oversight, our lack of attention to a common concern of most people indicated our mutual awareness that as two mixed-bloods we would stand out in the crowd and recognize each other instantly.

BLOOD BROTHERS: FIRST IMPRESSIONS

I was right. As soon as Hideo walked in we seemed to recognize each other, but he hesitated slightly before walking slowly toward my table. I took his show of uncertainty as a sign of shyness and reticence. I stood up, smiled, and said his name, and when he nodded, I said mine and offered my hand. He gave a weak smile and offered a hand obviously unused to the social custom of shaking. It was soft and limp like a lump of tofu and on this scorchingly hot summer day felt strangely cool.

When I felt his hand, my immediate thought was, "What a wimp!" I was certain he had been roughed up by bullies. My father had drilled into me the belief that I always had to be ready to fight. He sensed the trouble I was in for as the only Japanese kid in an American town where Japs were seen only in war movies that we were shown at the Boy's Club. I was fair game when the lights came on and the excited kids found a real live Jap in their midst. My dad had trained me with boxing lessons before sending me off to the Boy's Club, where tough kids were sure to be waiting for me. He was right; the bullies were there. But my boxing skills had carried me through my childhood. Once I had bloodied the face of one tormentor and sent him home crying, going to the Boy's Club became a lot easier.

I was sure no one had ever taught the young man in front of me how to fight. His dad certainly had not been around long enough to teach him how to survive the normal trials of being a boy. All Amerasians are vulnerable to teasing or being singled out as different, but whether they become targets of vicious bullying depends partly on the current political climate in Okinawa, where antimilitary feelings can easily be projected onto them. Bullying also depends largely on the personality characteristics of the individual child and Hideo looked like what other boys would call a sissy. He was shy, effeminate, and quiet with a lack of energy and confidence that he manifested in his facial expressions and body language. He seemed an obvious target of bullying. Sweeping these thoughts away, I offered him a seat, noting that therapy with another Amerasian would no doubt evoke feelings toward the client—in psychological jargon called countertransference—on a level that I had never experienced.

Hideo looked uncomfortable, not just from the heat but also I sensed from the tension he felt about the meeting. He offered just brief answers to my small talk about the weather and the town, so I asked him about his desire to engage in counseling.

"Yeah, my mother thinks I need counseling."

"What do you think?"

"I think I'd like to try it."

I was surprised to learn that Hideo had already been to a counselor, just a few months before. But it turned out that he had been just once, so I asked him why he had not gone back.

He paused a while before answering.

"She said she knew what the problem was, but she was wrong."

"And what did she say was the problem?"

"She said it was the bullying . . . but it's not."

"Your mother thinks so too?"

"Yeah."

"And what do you think is the problem?"

"I'm not sure."

"Well, what is bothering you the most now?"

A lengthy silence ensued until he finally spoke.

"I started working in a gas station, but I have trouble talking with people. I start to feel uncomfortable and feel like I want to get away. I think people are uncomfortable with me too."

Through more questioning I found out that after finishing junior high, Hideo had mostly stayed at home for the past 3 years, getting a high school diploma through night school. Now he had decided to take a part-time job and his anxieties had reemerged. He felt socially awkward and excessively nervous and didn't know how to reach out and make contact and open himself to people.

And he had a sense of urgency. He was approaching his 20th birthday—the ritual time of passage into adulthood in Japan. He felt that he did not want to become an adult in such bad shape and wished to change himself. I admired his courage and determination and wanted to support his efforts. I hoped that his desire to change by his next birthday and my imminent departure from Okinawa would give us the reality of a limited time frame that could work to our advantage by increasing the efficiency of therapy.

I suggested we meet once a week until the end of March, and then we could talk about whether to continue or not. In any case, I informed him that I would only be in Okinawa until September, when I would be returning to my job in Tokyo. That gave us only 6 months.

A BOY WITHOUT A SONG: THE LOSS OF JOY

Hideo seemed sad, withdrawn, uncommunicative, and weak. He had little ambition and energy. He was so dark and lifeless and without joy, and had so much difficulty speaking, that the image came to me of a boy without a song. When I was growing up my house was always filled with song, with my Irish father leading my older sisters and me in his and our favorite tunes. But there came the day in adolescence when, wallowing in melancholy, I refused to sing for my father, and it was years before I would sing for him again. Hideo looked like he had stopped singing a long time ago, and I wondered if he had ever started.

Since Hideo could not articulate what was bothering him, I was not sure where we would begin therapy. But from his report of his previous attempt at therapy, I knew where we would not begin. The therapist, perhaps influenced by the mother, had apparently been convinced from the start that the bullying in junior high school was the primary source of anxiety and that therapy must therefore begin from a discussion of that experience.

It seemed like a good guess. Bullying in junior high is known to be vicious and Amerasians are easy targets, visibly different and convenient scapegoats for the tensions locals hold toward their permanent military guests. And it would seem that the bullying had a long-term effect, as Hideo had been only marginally functional since junior high school.

Some therapists assess the client quickly, and decide what should be the focus of therapy. They view the client's disagreement with their agenda as refusal to cooperate and see their job as overcoming this resistance. However, in my view Hideo's previous therapist had simply hastened his departure since she had probably insisted on beginning therapy on a topic that Hideo had said was not the problem. To me, it doesn't matter what I think is the genesis of psychopathology or the primary source of anxiety; we begin therapy at the level of the client's concerns. My rule is that I always deal with what the client is offering me at the time. Otherwise, the client may correctly conclude that therapy is not for him and terminate without having begun. I believe that if something is truly important, it will come up at some point. So I suggested to Hideo that we talk about whatever he wanted and that maybe we could discover what was really bothering him.

I also wanted a chance to meet his mother, so I suggested that they come together for the next visit. Besides the insight into the nature of their relationship that her presence would provide, I was also hoping to be able to gather some background information, a painstakingly slow process with Hideo.

A MEETING WITH MOTHER

His mother turned out to be an attractive, talkative, and energetic woman beside whom Hideo seemed to shrink and become even more reserved and childlike. She spoke in an open and direct manner and answered my questions at length, without hesitation or embarrassment. Her flair and energy were in stark contrast to Hideo's depressive manner.

She described Hideo as a gentle and quiet baby who grew up normally. His only problem had been adjusting to Japanese school after transferring from English school when his father had left them and Okinawa. She blamed her husband, who couldn't understand Japanese and didn't like it when others spoke Japanese, so made the two of them speak English, at least when he was around. She also acknowledged her own shortcomings. "I was kind of depressed after my husband left us, so didn't give him as much attention as I should have. But he adjusted and liked going to school. That all changed when he got bullied in junior high school."

She described her husband as a typical military man who didn't show his feelings, and seemed most comfortable when he was drinking with his buddies. He was jealous of the attention she gave to Hideo, and they argued about that. "I told him it was just the Japanese way, but he said Hideo is American, so we should raise him like an American boy. Actually his name was Gregory at the time; I changed it when he got Japanese nationality."

Questions that I threw out to the two of them were always answered by her. When I directed the question to Hideo, there would be a long pause and then he would begin to speak with what appeared to be a laborious effort of getting his mouth into a condition capable of emitting sound. His answers were brief, but his mother would then pick up the ball and speak at length on the topic. The one statement of significance that Hideo was able to make that day was to counter his mother's assertion that bullying was the problem.

His mother also provided information about her own troubles of depression, hysteria, and anxiety. And when there is a depressed parent, there is a good chance there will be a depressed child, or one showing some other kind of emotional illness. I wondered how Hideo had been affected growing up with such a highly vulnerable mother. How much of his inexpressive emotional style was a reaction to a mother whose own needs were threatened by her child and who may not have responded warmly to his expression of needs? Had he learned early in life to shut down emotionally and to become withdrawn, stoic, and self-denying?

His mother had clearly had a hard time since meeting her ex-husband, a 19-year-old from Lubbock, Texas, in her job at a shop just outside the military base in Koza. They were both young and after a brief courtship had decided to live together. She spoke a little English, and he very little Japanese, but perhaps their inability to communicate had enhanced their romantic fantasies.

She described a struggle with depression over the past several years since the death of her mother, and appeared so needy that I wondered who should be in therapy, son or mother. Although family therapy with the mother might have been beneficial, because of Hideo's desire for individual therapy and his extreme difficulty of speaking in front of her, I decided to proceed privately, with the expectation that I might need to invite the mother in again at some point.

The meeting with Hideo's mother gave me a more complete picture. His father had been emotionally distant and a verbally and physically inexpressive man who maintained a formal relationship with his son. Young and needy himself, he had resented the attention Hideo received from his mother. But after being rejected by her family and abandoned by Hideo's father, she had probably turned to her son for emotional comfort and intimacy. As a result, Hideo's relationship with his mother had been exclusive, overly intimate, and prolonged in its closeness.

Hideo had missed school for a long time in junior high. Like most school-refusal children, he was very close to his mother and, of course, distant from his absent father. I assumed that these unclear generational boundaries had interfered with Hideo's developmental tasks of adolescence and his psychological separation from his mother. And the resolution of this conflict through identification with the father had not been possible for Hideo. His adolescence had been arrested in terms of the development of sexuality, autonomy, and social relations. It appeared equally hard for his mother to separate from her now-adolescent child.

LANGUAGE AND INTIMACY:
FACILITATING COMMUNICATION AND TRUST

Early in the next session we addressed the issue of language. An advantage of Japanese is that it has multiple levels of speech that indicate formality, respect, and distance so it can be informative to analyze the level of speech chosen by the client. However, English often enhances the freedom of expression in Japanese people by allowing levels of status and intimacy to remain ambiguous. In English Hideo wouldn't need to be concerned about such complications and could possibly communicate in a more uninhibited manner.

I hoped that Hideo's choice of English could also enable him to adopt a more open and revealing mode of behavior in which there was less expectation and reliance on nonverbal communication. In a Japanese mode, my position as a professor from an elite university, a clear hierarchical superior, would further block his expression of feelings and encourage him to expect me to be naturally sensitive and intuitively understanding. I think we both desired to free ourselves from some of the inhibitions and prohibitions associated with Japanese language and culture and as two bicultural persons, felt free to relate to each other in a more American way.

Although he could not say why he preferred it, I also assumed that English better represented the conflicts he was facing. I have found that Japanese clients often find it easier to express desires related to autonomy and freedom in English and I suspected that he had come to talk of these issues.

But despite our use of English, Hideo seemed restricted by cultural constraints. He seemed to feel highly vulnerable in a situation in which his inner world might be revealed. I felt that much of what I might expect many American clients to disclose was regarded by Hideo as private. Like other Japanese clients I have known, who were unused to expressing their inner selves in a spontaneous and unguarded fashion, Hideo kept these feelings and thoughts secret; if he expressed them at all, he did so only indirectly and subtly. Although I believed that the expression of these secrets would be powerful and important therapeutically, I expected them to emerge only after trust had been established and Hideo understood their importance in therapy. As he sensed that I was sufficiently empathic to pick up his innuendoes and cues, he would reveal more of his inner world.

And so I struggled to establish intimacy while still maintaining appropriate cultural boundaries. I wanted to encourage reflections and revelations, while not being too intrusive into what Hideo regarded as his private self by probing and interpreting. It seemed that despite our American mode of relating, we could not completely rid ourselves of more Japanese expectations, one being that too much probing could disrupt the warm and nurturing relationship between us.

Still, Hideo spoke so little that I was forced to become active. In doing so, I tried not to infantilize him and impose myself and my goals on him, but had to struggle to avoid becoming impatient and insisting that he too quickly or fully confront his feelings. I sensed that being too directive, misjudging the amount of pain he was in, would lead directly to resistance on his part. As with more active clients, I needed to maintain an attitude of guiding or helping him to unfold. I tried to sense his own instinctive understanding of what he needed for his healing.

But Hideo had a hard time explaining anything. I had to admit that he was a frustrating client, unable to express what he felt or what he wanted. He seemed wish-blocked and devoid of desires, impulses, opinions, inclinations; he did not seem to know what he felt or what he wanted. I began to wonder about the scholarly claim that Japanese people lack an authentic self. It could be some time, I thought, before he could articulate what was really bothering him, or trust me and therapy enough to be able to reveal the source of his anxiety. Although he was attuned to others' feelings, needs, and moods, he was insensitive to his own feelings and had little idea how to express them directly.

Hideo complained of having no emotions and no desires; therefore any actions were too much for him to attempt. He described feelings of being like a stranger, looking at others as though they were living in another world, one inaccessible to him. But Hideo desired to be a part of that world and the smiles and laughter of others made him envious. There was anger behind his calm demeanor. He felt powerless in his life and incapable of commitment to any options, all of which seemed unsatisfactory. He was trapped, plunged into darkness, and afraid to leave his small world.

But alienation can potentially serve as motivation for the pursuit of greater meaning and connection and new contexts for understanding. Now that Hideo had begun to reject how he clung to and yet despised his alienation, he could open to alternative ways of viewing the world and his place in it. This is the growth that I hoped to support as his therapist.

Searching for a foothold, I attempted to help him work on his life situation but made little progress. We talked about his work and focused on some cognitive and behavioral strategies he might try. But he seemed to resist any suggestions of how he might change his present situation, and after a few sessions the therapy seemed stuck.

BARING ONE'S SOUL: BREAKING THROUGH THE ICE

Then suddenly one day, shortly after he entered my office, he looked me in the eye, cleared his throat, and said, "I would like to ask you something. Is it normal for a mother to want to kiss her son on the lips?"

There are critical moments in therapy in which you feel as if you have entered into another realm of awareness—as though you have been granted admission to a private chamber in the client's inner and intimate world. Assumptions and stereotypes are blasted away in a flash of clarity. There is a new, heightened feeling of being with the client—barriers of consciousness evaporated and perceptions sharpened. I was struck silent by the power of Hideo's question. He did not ask it lightly but had obviously been bothered by it for a long time. I wondered how to answer him.

I tried to imagine his mother trying to kiss Hideo on the lips, but somehow couldn't picture it. If she had been Latina I could easily imagine it, but somehow the image of a Japanese woman kissing her grown son on the lips seemed too incongruous to me.

Hideo was looking at me expectantly, and waiting for my answer. Now what did he want me say? Was he simply asking me as a professional psychologist to confirm his suspicions that his mother was acting a little strange? Or to assert that she was normal? Was he releasing a family secret from its cage, hoping to dispel its power over him? Could it be that he had never been able to ask another person this strange question? I felt I needed to clarify the situation before passing judgment. But first I wanted to acknowledge Hideo's disclosure. This was clearly a turning point in therapy and I wanted Hideo to realize the importance of what he had dared to do.

"I suppose it's hard for you to ask that question."

Hideo hesitated before saying, "I guess it has bothered me, but I couldn't ask anyone about it."

"Well, this kind of family situation can be hard to talk about, maybe embarrassing for you or for your mother."

Hideo nodded as if he understood that I understood.

"I appreciate your sharing this with me. And how does it make you feel?"

"A little uncomfortable."

"Have you ever told her that?"

"Yeah, I told her but she just says 'I can't help it . . . I love you . . . Your father's American . . . We don't have to do the Japanese way, we're Okinawan!' She just says a lot of things that don't make any sense."

"So she didn't seem to understand that it upsets you?"

Hideo nodded.

"Well, I guess a lot depends on the age of the children, and generally when kids reach puberty mothers aren't as physical with their sons. In some countries, it's more normal to hug and kiss. I don't know about Okinawa, but in other parts of Japan where I have lived, I've never heard of mothers kissing kids on the lips. I think that most mothers, once boys are no longer little, become more reserved in their touching. It's a way of recognizing that the boy has grown up."

I could tell by the look on his face that Hideo wanted me to say more. I was concerned with how he felt about his mother's behavior and her awareness of his feelings. Whether kissing a male child on the lips should be classified as an abnormal activity in Okinawa was less important to me than the fact that it made him very uncomfortable and yet his mother persisted in doing it and Hideo protested only mildly.

So I told him, "I guess the important thing is that it makes you uncomfortable; I think a lot of people would feel the same. It would have made me uncomfortable at your age if my mother had tried to kiss me on the lips."

I wondered what was behind his question. Why was he so bothered by his mother's behavior? Was it excessive or provocative? He seemed lost in thought for a while, then more came out.

"She acts like that in public too. Even when people are around she still tries to hug and kiss me."

"And that also makes you uncomfortable?"

Hideo nodded.

After her husband's escape, his mother, faced with the responsibility of supporting herself and her 8-year-old son, took a job as a bar hostess. It paid far better than working in a shop and she wasn't qualified for much else. Perhaps the expression of sexuality that was required at her job was what disturbed her son so much when she brought it home from work with her.

I felt that Hideo was like many other people who enter therapy with the disturbing notion that they are the only person who has certain frightening or unacceptable problems, thoughts, impulses, or fantasies. This sense of being alone and unique in their suffering is heightened for those like Hideo who are socially isolated. In his solitary world he was neither able to learn about others' similar feelings and experiences nor able to confide in and be validated and accepted by others.

Although I had to acknowledge his feeling that his mother's behavior was excessive, I also wanted Hideo to realize that the confusing intimacy of mother-son relations was a universal human drama. Since he had limited knowledge of the field of psychology, I told him how the Oedipus complex speaks to the heart of the complexity of mother-son relations. He was curious so I further explained that some Japanese psychoanalysts claim that the Ajase complex, taken from a Buddhist myth, is more central to the Japanese psyche. While the Oedipus complex is about the mother-father-son triangle, the Ajase complex focuses on the mother-son dyad in portraying a son who rages over feelings of loss of their symbiotic tie, only to repent later after he realizes the great sacrifices his mother makes for him. I reminded him that he was not the only Japanese boy who was disturbed by the sense of sexuality between himself and his mother, and that I had personally known several similar cases.

I was sure that Hideo would feel relief from knowing that he was not the only person who had such strange and disturbing things happen to him. His disclosure would be liberating and enable him to feel more in touch with the world. To know that his most shameful or unspeakable thoughts or actions were not outside the experience of other people should make him feel more human. It has always amazed me in therapy what a great relief it is to people to simply discover that they are not alone, that others share the same dilemmas and life experiences.

I could now understand why Hideo had insisted that the bullying was not the problem. He had resisted his mother's and his previous therapist's attempts to begin therapy there because he knew that he was more concerned about something else. But at that time he was either unable or unwilling to articulate his concern. I assumed that his simple question revealed a far deeper fear of the erotic tension between him and his mother, and of her refusal to treat him as the young man he had become.

HIS GAIN IS HER PAIN

In the following sessions, Hideo began to slowly express more concerns. Although he could still not talk at length, he came prepared to ask a question or introduce a topic. Now that he had been able to ask the big question that had been bothering him, Hideo started to recall other incidents.

"Last year there was a girl at my part-time job who was very friendly and would talk to me sometimes. We live in the same part of town, so we started going home together. One night after work she asked me to go out with her to a coffee shop. I called my mother to tell her I would be home late, because that was her night off from work. But when I got back around 1:00 and she was still up and acting really strange and angry and was crying. She kept repeating something like, "How can you make your mother worry about you?'"

"How did you feel?"

"I felt very strange. I hadn't done anything wrong; she wasn't even my girlfriend."

"Would it have been wrong if it had been your girlfriend?"

"I guess not . . . I don't know . . . I've never had a girlfriend."

"Would you like to?"

"Maybe I'd like to try someday."

"Does anything hold you back from trying?"

"It's just hard to talk to anyone."

The next week Hideo revealed another story.

"When I was little my mom would take me to the beach near my grandparents' house during summer vacation. One day a little girl started to talk to me and asked me to build a sand castle with her. So I played with her for a while. But my mother called me and when I went back to where she was sitting under the parasol, she seemed upset and asked me questions about the girl and why I was playing with her and things like that. She acted like she was angry but I couldn't understand why."

"Why do you think she may have been angry?"

"I don't know."

"Did you think that maybe she was jealous? I mean, maybe she felt that you were everything to her and she didn't want anyone else to have you."

Hideo didn't answer but after seeming lost in thought recalled more of his feelings when his father left. His mother had retreated to her room and, left alone, Hideo had followed her there. They comforted each other in their loneliness and he had returned to sleep in the bedroom that he had been removed from at his father's insistence that a couple's bedroom was no place for a child.

Hideo began to paint a picture of a young man wary of competition with men and inordinately shy of women. He seemed afraid to do anything, as experiences of joy, especially those with girls, threatened the relationship of mother and son. Attempting to find pleasure was associated with inflicting pain on his mother. He was put into the seemingly impossible position that if he was happy, it made his mother unhappy. Therefore, if he sacrificed himself he could maintain his mother's equilibrium. The secret to his depression and lifelessness seemed to lie in this dilemma he faced. His suffering was related directly now to his failure to grow as a young male. He was afraid of his own sexuality.

FINDING VOICE: GAINING INSIGHT

I wanted Hideo to realize this connection between his lack of feelings and his twisted relationship with his mother, but it was painstaking work. Although he began to recall various experiences and feelings, he made no connections between those earlier events and his present situation. As with many clients, Hideo's lack of psychological-mindedness made self-analysis difficult. My interpretations usually seemed clear to me, but when I attempted to explain them, I found them hopelessly confusing to Hideo. And a therapist's explanations and interpretations, no matter how good, have meaning only if they make sense to the client. Despite our best intentions to teach, clients, like everyone else, learn the most from truth they discover themselves. Therefore, I tried to contain the intellectual excitement generated by my insightful interpretations and to be patient and offer them at the right moment to Hideo in a more creative manner.

As explanations and interpretations were of limited value, I thought that Hideo could benefit from actually trying the behaviors he feared and observing his feelings. So I asked him to take small steps in doing what he wanted to do. His actions would then make his mother angry and he could observe and modulate his own reactions to his mother's emotions. But Hideo let me know that I was moving too quickly. He was too lifeless to do anything, he claimed. So I tried in various ways to encourage him to explore his lack of joy and energy.

"You know Hideo, I feel that you are sad, but I don't know the source of this sadness. What do you think it is?"

"I don't know. I don't think I feel sad. I don't feel anything."

He often responded in this manner, so I had started to verbally reflect or mirror what I sensed he was feeling or thinking, allowing him to confirm or correct me. Therapy with Hideo included educating him about internal mental processes. Whenever possible, I also resorted to humor, and delighted in the rare but increasingly more common occasions when my use of levity could bring a smile to Hideo's solemn face.

"You strike me as somewhat lifeless, without energy or enjoyment. Maybe it's related to what we talked about before. When you discovered that your actions make your mother unhappy, you stopped doing those things, as a kind of way of showing love. So your activity level gradually decreased from lack of reinforcement. You learned to be helpless, because you felt that no matter what you did, it resulted in unhappiness."

Hideo seemed to be digesting what I was saying, but didn't respond. I tried a different approach.

"What would you say makes you happy?"

Still no response. These were hard questions for him.

So I said, "I'm asking you because in some ways I was a lot like you when I was younger. There was a time when I was a little lifeless but I realized that I didn't know the cause. I began to see that I had taken on my father's sadness; just to share it with him. Maybe you're doing something like that."

Hideo appeared to listen intently to my self-revelation. And as he often did, Hideo considered my words for a long time before responding. I had learned to allow long periods of silence for him to digest, reflect on, and react to my words.

Finally he said, "Sometimes my mother just curls up in a ball and doesn't move. After my dad left I didn't go to school for a while. I had been going to the school on the military base, but they told me because my dad was no longer in the military I couldn't go there any more. But I guess my mom didn't register me at the public school, so I just stayed home until my aunt took me over one day. My mom wasn't even going out of the house . . . sometimes she still does that . . . starts crying and doesn't talk."

"There seems to be a lot of unhappiness there. Maybe you decided to take on some of that sadness," I suggested. "I think kids do that for their parents, to share it, to lighten the load. It's a form of love. But the problem is that the load can become too heavy for the kid."

"I don't know . . . I don't remember deciding to do that."

"It's just a possible explanation. This is the way psychologists think. There is a belief that there is an unconscious, a part of us that is removed from our ordinary consciousness. Therefore, we are not always aware of all our thoughts and feelings. So even if you are not aware of thinking like this, these things are going on inside you, out of conscious thought. If this way of thinking doesn't make sense to you, don't worry about it. Just consider that it is one possible way of understanding and explaining the way the mind works."

Our goal in therapy was set by Hideo at the beginning when he asserted his desire to become more autonomous. And it was obvious that this involved creating distance in the mother-child relationship. He seemed fixed at a stage of early mother attachment, dependent on her and helpless, passive, and receptive. He sorely lacked the qualities of independence and mastery of the social world, which children often learn from fathers. His loving but overindulgent and domineering mother had been driven by her own need for love to possessiveness and refusal to bear the necessary and inevitable separation from her growing child. And through his identification with and empathy for his mother, Hideo had been released from his aloneness, but trapped in a prison from which he struggled to escape.

SURVIVAL NARRATIVES: CULTURAL CONSIDERATIONS OF WHAT'S NORMAL

I did not take on the work of separating parent and child lightly. Although in Hideo's case the need for separation seemed obvious, I am wary of my own cultural assumptions. Despite my immersion in specialized multicultural clinical training, much of what I learned in mainstream psychology and through socialization in the United States I have had to view as biased and ethnocentric and often not representative of many other cultures of the world.

Psychology defines a developmental task of adolescence as a quest for autonomy marked by successfully separating from one's family. Helping adolescents achieve a healthy independence is therefore simply assumed to be an appropriate goal for therapy. However, the automatic insistence of psychotherapists that separation from family is a necessary solution for growth may end up depriving people of the very source of support that they most need. I wanted Hideo to push his mother away without destroying the bond.

The mother-son relationship in Japan is often described as especially intimate and *amae* theory also asserts the importance of healthy forms of experiencing and expressing dependency needs. Studies of mother-infant interaction indicate that Japanese tend to see the infant's development in terms of becoming increasingly interdependent with others. In comparison, Americans seem to see the infant's development as becoming increasingly independent of others. So what is a normative emotional distance in a mother-child relationship? Does it matter that the mother is Japanese and the child is American-Japanese? Would encouraging independence be an American cultural assumption? Would encouraging dependence be Japanese? And how did these cultural assumptions influence what I should regard as normal and abnormal development and how I formulated goals in therapy?

After considering cultural assumptions, a therapist must make a judgment. Although a high level of intimacy may be the norm in Japan, in recent years there is concern that in too many families the level of intimacy between mother and child, and sons in particular, has become extreme. As in Hideo's case, these relations form part of an unbalanced and dysfunctional family pattern that is characterized by social and psychological problems of adolescents. These days the phrase "mother complex" has become part of common vocabulary and portrays these mother-son relationships that have gone beyond Japanese cultural norms.

And Hideo was being clear that he was disturbed that the relationship felt too close for him. I viewed Hideo's symbiotic tie with his mother as a way of guarding himself against the anxiety inherent in individuation. But this defensive strategy succeeds only temporarily, and then becomes a source of secondary anxiety. For Hideo, bullying was ostensibly the trigger in seeking therapy, but I was increasingly convinced that his reluctance to separate from his mother had interfered with his attendance at school and the development of social skills, and led to his retarded growth and self-contempt.

I believed that claiming his separateness would bring an awareness of his aloneness, and therefore full responsibility for his own life. He needed to accept the consequences that followed from his actions and open himself to the possibility of deep intimate connections with self and others. Only by embracing all his sensual and emotional intimacies could he discover the yearnings of his soul.

SHARING STORIES

Although the theme of separation and autonomy constituted the content of our dialogue, I felt that my best chance to help Hideo lay in the development of a meaningful relationship with him. I assumed he had come to me not only for self-exploration to deal with his problems but also for what the relationship itself could provide. I hoped that the establishment of an intimate bond with me might sufficiently attenuate his bond with his mother so that he could begin to pry himself loose from her. Then I thought we could turn to the identification and removal of obstacles that were preventing him from establishing intimate relationships in his social life.

Being Amerasian like Hideo was part of what I offered. It had drawn him to approach me and filled him with expectations of shared understanding that I knew realistically did not always exist. The reflection of our own human struggles was heightened as we faced each other.

But how these connections would be useful in therapy I still did not know. Hideo had experienced deep and unresolved pain but had little conscious awareness of these feelings of fear, embarrassment, grief, and anger. He was overdistanced from his emotions, and I felt I needed to bring him closer to them to enable him to experience and work through them, to achieve catharsis and an aesthetic distance from his original experience. But how?

Working on overcoming blocked feelings can be incredibly slow and demanding. Some therapists go for instant and powerful breakthroughs by blasting through defenses and confronting the client with his or her feelings. However, such methods may not lead to long-term change and may also create disturbing side-effects. I tried instead the less dramatic process of constantly asking Hideo how he felt, to help him explore the nature of his stifled feelings. He often was able to acknowledge that he had feelings and to examine what was blocking them. When this failed to generate a response, I would ask him how he felt about being asked how he felt.

But with a time limit on our therapy facing us, I searched for some way to move the process along more quickly. I reflected on my initial reaction to Hideo's effeminate behavior. Why had I felt turned off, even contemptuous? Why had it triggered memories of childhood violence in which I triumphed by being tough? I became more aware of my narrative of survival. But had it really happened as I thought? Yes, I had fought and bloodied and vanquished my tormentor, but wasn't it in a boxing ring with gloves, and not on the street? And had going to the Boy's Club really gotten easier? Weren't there always new tormentors every time I went? Yes, I had refused to be cowed and continued to go there, but wasn't I always filled with a dread that at any moment I would be taunted and engulfed in violence?

I wondered why I had succumbed to this romanticization of my youth. Some years earlier in therapy, as I sought to rid myself of the confines of my narrative of victimization, I had seized on the realization that although I had been harassed and hurt I had never been defeated. I had not allowed myself to be intimidated and had faced the bullies and won. Although the racial slurs were hurled, they came from faceless mobs who dared not to lay a hand on me.

We all construct stories, or narratives, of our lives to make sense of them. And I had constructed a new narrative, truly romantic, as a tough and stoic kid who had triumphed over the slings and arrows of racial prejudice. Now did it matter that my story may not have been historically correct? On the other hand, was it possible to even discover the historical truth? Or did truth change according to the perspective of the observer?

I wondered how I could help Hideo to feel more and to construct a new narrative. In his present tragic narrative, Hideo was a victim of his possessive mother, of his irresponsible father, of his distant grandparents, and of his vicious racial antagonists. But he was also a survivor and he was still trying to live as best he could.

Before constructing this new narrative, Hideo first needed to get closer to his emotions. Perhaps I could help him by asking him to remember what it was like being attacked, called names, losing face; being unable to fight back; feeling terror, humiliation, anger. He might resist my attempts, but I thought he would respond because of our shared culture and experience. After all, I had lived this myself, it was genuinely a part of me, not knowledge from a book. It was worth a try.

"You know that there may be something about the bullying too that is related to your deadening of emotions. You haven't talked about it but I know that when I was attacked it left me deadened in a way as a way of coping with it."

Hideo seemed surprised at the mention of my personal experience, and very interested.

"Did you have any experience of bullying growing up in the United States?"

"Sure, many times. I guess a lot of kids growing up here assume that in the United States there is no discrimination toward Amerasians, but it depends on where you live. I grew up in a completely White town, so I stood out. And it wasn't so long after the end of the war. I was called names a lot, like jap, chink, ching chong chinaman. Maybe it wasn't so severe, but it hurt me a lot when I was little. I couldn't understand how people could hate me just because I was Japanese."

Surprisingly, I felt my emotions surging and my voice wavering just to recall these experiences. But Hideo was with me and after we sat in silence for a while, responded with his own story.

"Kids used to attack me on the way home from school. They would be waiting for me outside the school gate. One day there was a rumor at school that an American GI had killed an Okinawan woman with a knife. After school, there was a big gang waiting for me. They started calling me names: Hijami, that means goat's eyes in Okinawan. They told me to go home to America. That was weird—I've never even been to America. They threatened to cut me up too. I tried to pretend I didn't hear them and just kept walking. But they bumped me and pushed me. I was scared.

"Then I felt a rock hit the side of my face. I put my hand up to my head and felt the warm blood oozing out. It hurt but I still didn't show any reaction, just kept walking. Then more rocks hit me and they started running after me, I became terrified and ran like crazy. I got to my house before them and rushed inside. I slammed the door and could hear them outside for a while, but they went away. I just sat there on the floor for a long time, shaking and crying."

Hideo was moved almost to tears by recounting his childhood trauma. He seemed so human and so vulnerable. I was deeply touched. I hesitated to probe, but felt that this moment could be a breakthrough and so decided to ask him to explore it further.

"How old were you?"

"I was 12 . . . in junior high. It was my first year."

"Do you remember how you felt besides being scared?"

"I guess I just couldn't understand why it happened. . . . It seemed unfair. . . . I hadn't done anything. . . . Why did they have to pick on me?"

"When you recall the story now, it still seems raw. . . . I wonder what strikes you about it now?"

"I'm embarrassed how much it seems to have affected me. I tried to push it aside and act like it is in the past, but it was something that affected me a lot."

Then Hideo then looked up into my eyes and gave the most succinct expression of his pain.

"It hurts the heart."

His simple expression was so poignant that it made me wince, and we settled into a shared moment of silent commiseration. Sometimes his less than perfect English created striking poetic images. Hideo seemed exhausted, but the use of this strategic metaphor of racial violence had enabled him to gain access to feelings that he denied when asked directly about them. Our shared culture had allowed me to develop a therapeutic metaphor that might have been very difficult for a therapist from another background to use. After that we were able to talk about the anger and other feelings generated by the bullying. I tried to help him to not only deal with the feelings that were coming up, but also to put his experience into the wider social context of Amerasian experience in general and also of Okinawa as a breeding ground for prejudice.

Having finally talked about the bullying he had endured in junior high school also led to talking about being mixed. It had always been a source of pain and confusion for him and I could see that his alienation had also been aggravated by his experiences of racial difference. Once he transferred to public school, in his completely Japanese neighborhood and Japanese school, he was different from others, racially and culturally—not just different, but "American." He was also fatherless, and these were differences that made him the butt of antagonism and contempt and contributed to his excessive self-consciousness and emotional isolation. Hideo asked me how I felt about being mixed, and as always I tried to answer his question as openly and clearly as I could.

"I guess it's always concerned me more than some people. When I was younger there were times when it bothered me a lot. Being called names was hard, but I think I learned as a kid that we can't control the way others look at us. We just have to accept the way some people will look down on us. The only thing we can control is our own self-respect, what we think of ourselves. Meeting other Amerasians has really helped me to come to terms with it. To me being mixed was something that I wanted to explore. That's why I came back to Japan. I wanted to really have both sides of my heritage."

Hideo asked, "Where do you feel more at home, in Japan or the United States?"

"In a way I have always felt Japan is my home, since I was born here. But in other ways I have felt like a stranger, especially in the way that I am always regarded as a foreigner. I lived in the States for a long time, so I'm also at home there, but for some reason I choose to live here."

I had gone on long enough, and tried to bring the focus back to him. "How about you? You've told me a little about it already, but do you still feel it is hard to be mixed?"

"It was hard when I was younger and kids would call me names. Junior high was the worst, because I was actually attacked and bullied. I felt like some people looked at me like I represented the American military or something. If there was some demonstration against the military bases, some kids would look at me as if I was bad or I was the enemy. Even some of my teachers I don't think treated me fairly. When I did well in English they just said, 'Of course, after all you're American.' I had a fantasy that if we could only live with my dad in the United States everything would be better."

Ah, yes, the Amerasian fantasy. Those in Japan dream that life in the United States would be better; those in the United States dream that life in Japan would be better. There is always the allure of the illusion of the great escape across the sea when things get rough.

"I guess what's harder though was that even my family would say things. If I did something bad, it was always, 'See, you're American!' It was like they were saying I was bad because I was American. Even my grandmother would say that kind of thing. . . . I always thought she loved my cousins more than me."

Having grown up with two loving families, one Irish and one Japanese, I sympathized with Hideo's situation. He had never had his father's family and the attitudes of his mother's family had really hurt him; to know that he was loved less, just because he was part American. I only knew this rejection from outsiders, not from anyone within my family. His pain showed.

GOING TO AMERICA: ESCAPE OR CHALLENGE?

We sat in silence for a while, but Hideo broke it by announcing, "I've thought about going to the United States."

Now this was a surprise! "Since when?"

"Well, I've thought about it a long time but just recently began to feel that I really want to go."

"I can understand your desire to go, but what would you want to do there?"

"I'm not sure, but maybe it's like you described for yourself, only the opposite. I mean, I'm mixed Japanese and American, but I've never even lived in the United States. I don't know much about it—the culture and society and people. I think I'd just like to experience living there."

"What do you think you might discover there?"

"I don't know . . . maybe something new about myself. . . . I don't know, it's hard for me to imagine. I've wanted to go for a long time. I always felt it's my country too, in a way. But I've always been embarrassed that even though people think I'm American I don't really know anything about America. So I thought if I went there and lived there and learned the language better and what Americans are like, maybe I would have more self-confidence."

"Well, I think you're right, it could work for you in that way. I think of it as empowerment. Enabling ourselves to claim a heritage requires hard work—such as a journey home, language and cultural study, and experiencing daily life in the culture. An expression I like for this process is 'identity won in action.'"

I encouraged him to come up with a concrete plan for such a trip, and to prepare for it so that he could get the most out of it. I offered to help him in any way I could, but I thought it was important for him to do the investigation and legwork to demonstrate his will to act. I felt there was more to this trip than what he was saying. Surely he must have the desire to see his father, I thought, but decided to wait to see if he brought it up.

In the meantime we returned to Hideo's relationship with his mother. I tried to help him again to see the tragic narrative he had developed as the hero who must suffer to save his mother. His happiness must be sacrificed so that she can live. The bullying that he endured also drove him further into isolation with his mother, and therefore allowed him to fulfill her emotional needs. He had become the martyr who gives up his life to accompany the mother, alone and forsaken.

USING STORIES TO TEACH: METAPHORS OF GROWTH AND DEVELOPMENT

I wanted to help Hideo break open this story to make possible his telling a new story. I hoped he could transform himself by reshaping the story of how his life was connected from past to present to future, and develop a new way of valuing the past and imagining the future. Hideo needed to construct a new narrative, to view his life in a different way.

To begin to do this, I sensed that Hideo needed to act. I encouraged him to force himself to attempt small acts that might bring him pleasure and to observe his reactions. I hoped he could experience himself and his choices. And as he acted, what emerged from these trials were realizations of motives for his actions. Hideo had the sense of possessing a part of his life that had seemed lost.

He recalled his mother's telling him that if he was bad his father would go away. The night before his father left he had pouted when told to eat his carrots, angering his father. Hideo was sure that this was the reason his father had left. And then he feared that if he was bad his mother too might leave. Or that he might even kill her by making her worry.

He began to see the way in which his dread of hurting his mother had led him to his present state of death in life. Each act of assertion that he now attempted brought anxiety, but Hideo also learned to tolerate the ever widening gulf between himself and his mother. He came to see his own role in perpetuating his outlook and realized that he had the power to change. As he recognized that he himself was responsible for his life and the one in control, his helplessness faded and he felt a surge of desire to live. As Hideo accepted that he himself had brought on his trouble and resolved to change, he evolved from tragic hero to romantic hero.

I tried to introduce stories that would contain powerful metaphors that might touch him deeply, as the one about racial violence in childhood had. Since Hideo had been raised as a Christian and throughout his life had attended church, I related the story of Jesus that had inspired me as a young man trying to gather the courage to leave home and go out into the world. Because I left the church nearly 30 years ago, my recollection was a little vague, but I still remembered the basic story.

"What you're going through reminds me of the story of the young Jesus, and how he disappears. Have you heard it?"

Hideo shook his head.

"Well, Jesus is a teenager and he disappears one day, so his parents go out looking for him. At last his mother discovers him talking with the wise men in the temple. She gives him a hard time, telling him how worried she was and so on. But Jesus is unmoved by her show of emotion and calmly informs her, 'But mother, did you not know that I must be about my father's work?'"

Hideo said, "Yeah, I remember that story now. I was worried that Jesus really upset Mary."

Of course you were, I thought. I decided to tell him something even closer to home. "I don't know if this will mean anything to you, but it is something that has stayed with me. I remember when I was about your age and my father said to me, 'Steve, don't let your mother drive you crazy.' I assumed that he meant that a mother's love can be enveloping and comforting but also smothering and that as a growing boy I needed to distance myself from it."

Hideo nodded as if he understood the point of the story.

"When you think of separating from your mother, what do you think you are afraid of?"

"I think I'm afraid that she will fall apart."

"Because she seems so fragile?"

Hideo nodded.

"You know, I think your mother is a lot stronger than you give her credit for. She's been through a lot. And we're not talking about abandoning her; you won't do that, your love is too strong. We're talking about learning to rely on her less, to allow others to be important to you, close to you. That would free your mother to do the same. But I think she needs you to make the first move."

Hideo looked at me as if pleading, "Is there no other way?" But I felt that I needed to drive the point home.

"When two people are stuck together and you try to separate them it is going to cause some pain. But unless they separate they can't continue to grow. For you to grow up you have to cause your mother pain. There is no other way. But these wounds heal."

An image came to me from my gardening, so I continued, "It's like when you have two plants growing close together they stunt each other's growth. But if you move them a little apart they both have a chance to thrive."

Hideo's blank look told me I had wasted a good nature metaphor on a city boy who had obviously never grown anything. I couldn't think of a better metaphor for him, so I just said, "It's the nature of a mother's love, to give and then to let go. Your mother's challenge now is to let go. Your independence is for your mother's sake as well. And a child's difficult reality is that he must eventually separate from the one who raises him; and in doing so he can't help but inflict pain on his mother."

Hideo was quieter than usual today, and I felt like sharing my experiences so continued to talk. "You know I am an only son too and I think I had a hard time separating from my mother. I went through something like what you are going through now. I know it's not easy. But one thing I learned is that my mother wanted me to grow up too. Even though it's painful to separate, she knew, as I think all mothers do, that it is natural. They won't be around forever, so they need us to become independent."

Therapists usually learn in training not to share personal information. Perhaps for some therapists this is a necessary rule to abide by. Many rationalizations are given for not sharing personal matters with clients, especially that time is valuable and that it is the client's therapy not the counselor's. Abuse of this technique no doubt occurs, but I have found that judicious sharing of myself and my experiences has helped clients. They have often told me how much they appreciated such revelations and how they were key aspects of therapy for them. Perhaps the awareness that the therapist must also struggle with and resolve personal problems provides them with a sense of a shared journey that lowers their resistance to revealing their problems.

Clients have let me know how much they want to hear about my personal life, and usually it is not very much. If they do want to hear a lot, it is a warning that they are avoiding facing their own issues. Generally, a little personal information goes a long way. My rule is to keep it brief, and return the focus quickly to the client. With Hideo I stretched this rule, not only because he was so silent and reticent, but because he seemed so moved by my personal stories and they in turn powerfully elicited his stories.

FINDING FATHER

While sharing my experience helped therapy to progress, Hideo had lived in fear of hurting his mother for so long that it was not a quick process to break this pattern. We returned to this theme many times. But Hideo began to make moves in his life, joining an English class, attending social gatherings at church, and reading more about the United States. In therapy he became even more active in bringing up new subjects, including his father.

"I think now being mixed is not so hard. Even though some people might not like me, in a way it's even a good thing because I have more than one cultural heritage. But I guess what's harder is knowing that I was not wanted . . . that my father didn't want me."

"Why do you say he didn't want you?"

"Because he left me."

"But do you know why he left?"

"No, I never understood why he left. I just remember coming home from school one day and finding my mother on the floor sobbing, all rolled up in a ball. My aunt was there trying to comfort her. She took me aside and told me that my father had left. I guess I was kind of in shock or something and I think I went to their bedroom and opened the closet and drawers to look for my father's things. Then I went to the front door, and that's where it really hit me, because all my dad's big shoes and boots were gone."

Jesus, I thought, the big son of a bitch didn't even say good-bye to his kid! I kept this thought to myself though, and instead asked him, "Where did he go?"

"I found out later he went back to the United States. My mom never really explained what happened."

"Did you ever hear from him?"

"No, he never wrote."

"I guess that must have been pretty hard for you as a little kid."

Hideo didn't answer, just nodded, as if in acknowledgment of his suffering as a child, then shrugged his shoulders.

"Can you remember any other feelings you had at that moment?"

"No, because I think I was numb . . . it was kind of unreal . . . like a bad dream."

"What about now when you think back on it?"

"I guess it was building for a long time, but I didn't know it."

Having seen the misery they have caused to countless innocent lives, I have a harsh attitude toward men who father children and casually leave them behind. I just took it for granted that my father had raised me—that's what fathers are supposed to do. But when I realized how many men had not done the same, I appreciated my father more just for staying with me.

I recalled a scene from childhood, walking down Main Street with my Irish aunt. A big man stopped us and asked about my dad. My Aunt Margaret told him that he was back from Japan, and glancing down at me said, "This is his son." A big grin came to his face and he said, "I've got a few kids back there myself." Aunt Margaret stiffened at his words, looked him hard in the eye, and said, "Well, my brother's not like that." And she pulled me by the hand and we walked away from that man.

Surely as a child Hideo had experienced rage and disappointment in his father after being abandoned without a word—and perhaps blamed himself for driving his father away. He had lived with dreams of his father's return as well as a growing stoic acceptance that he never would, when his army boots failed to appear again by the front door. But gradually he had learned to make peace with the past. My heart went out to him and I wished I could comfort him.

"You know, usually the reasons for leaving have more to do with the problems between the couple than the children. Your dad left because he and your mom couldn't get along; it wasn't because of you. Maybe you need to forgive yourself for something you didn't cause."

Hideo looked at me with a puzzled expression.

"I mean little kids often imagine that they have somehow caused their father to go away, by being bad or unlovable. Maybe you did that to yourself."

He didn't answer, and now that we were on the topic, I decided to bring up something that I had been waiting in vain for Hideo to broach.

"Do you think you might want to meet your father?"

"I've thought about it for a long time. I didn't say so before, but I think one of the big reasons I want to go to America is to meet my father."

"What do you think it might be like to meet him?"

"I guess it would be pretty strange. I haven't seen him for more than 10 years. It's hard to imagine."

"What do you think could go wrong? I mean, what are you afraid might happen?"

"I think what if he doesn't want to see me?"

"You realize that he may be remarried with a family now. And that he may not be what you have fantasized."

Hideo nodded.

"What are your feelings toward your father now?"

"I don't know. I guess I'm not angry any more. I don't expect anything from him, and I don't want to cause him any trouble. But I just want to meet him once."

I wanted to prepare him for what could happen and for him to learn about his vulnerabilities. I wholeheartedly supported his desire to meet his father, but I wanted Hideo to be aware of the scenario he would probably face. I offered to introduce him to other young Amerasians who had told me of their experience in searching for and finding their fathers. At least he would have a better idea of what to expect, a realistic sense of what awaited him. I imagined a young lifetime of fantasies exploded in a moment of brutal reality. Better to temper those dreams first with a dose of sober realism.

But not too much. Hideo had allowed himself to dream and to desire and he needed to continue to let his feelings blossom. When he had insisted at the beginning of therapy that he felt dead inside, I had assured him that he had feelings, but suggested that maybe it's too painful to feel; that maybe the pain gets short-circuited and put onto other things. I warned him that if he can't feel pain he won't feel anything else either.

HIDEO THE ADVENTURER

Through the course of counseling, Hideo had gradually begun to emerge from his shell and recognize and speak of feelings. He began to develop his desires. He talked of traveling, and more significantly, followed through on searching for his father's whereabouts. He talked of going to college and of eventually making enough money to live on his own. I felt as if I was witnessing the rebirth of *la joie de vivre*.

Hideo finally talked of moving out of his mother's home and living alone and I encouraged him to do it. He had moments of doubt. Could he do something that would lead to his mother's unhappiness? But I encouraged him to try to discuss these feelings with his mother and attempt to gain her understanding and approval. I offered to help facilitate their talking if he wished.

At this point I had to return to Tokyo temporarily and arranged to meet with Hideo on my return. When we met 6 weeks later, Hideo was unusually animated. As soon as he sat down, he announced, "I went to see my dad."

I was stunned and waited impatiently for him to explain what had happened.

"I had a vacation coming and suddenly decided to visit a cousin in Los Angeles. When I got there, we started talking and he said, 'Why don't you go to see your dad?' So I did it. I called his house. When I told him who I was, he became silent. I told him I just wanted to meet him once, and he said he would like to meet me too. So I went to his house."

"So what was it like?"

"It was like it was for other people, like everyone had told me. He didn't seem like my dad, I mean, I couldn't believe that this was my father. I just didn't feel anything special, like I thought I might. He was just like a nice middle-aged American man, like one of those guys you see on American television programs, kind of bald and fat."

I was sorry that Hideo had been disappointed, but how many happy endings to this story are there? Everyone I know who has searched for and found a long-lost father has told me of similar feelings.

"I was worried about disturbing him, and disrupting his life. But he explained that he lived alone now. He had married, but was divorced a few years ago. He said he never had any other kids, so I guess that makes me his only child.

"I wanted to ask him why he left us, but couldn't. But without my saying anything, he told me he was sorry that he had left me and my mother. He said they just couldn't get along and he found it hard to live in Japan. After he had come back to the United States he figured it was better not to bother us. I had a lot of other questions I wanted to ask him but mostly I just listened to him. Then he asked me about my plans for the future and I told him I wanted to go to college."

Hideo seemed to savor his words and to deliberately slow down his already normally ponderous pace of talking to maintain the suspense. I felt like sticking a pin in him to make him speak faster. But in the midst of my irritation, I suddenly realized with joy that Hideo was actually teasing me, and demonstrating an ability that for him was a great stride forward in his human relations.

Finally he blurted out, "And he offered to help me. He said there is a community college in his town and that he could help me to go there. He is tough though. He told me he will continue to pay my tuition only if I get decent grades."

"Wow, so what are you going to do?"

"I decided to go. I don't know what it will be like, but I'm going to try to go to school in America and live near my dad for a while."

I was amazed. It was more than I, and even Hideo, could have expected. Of course, there had been no romantic and dramatic reunion like in a movie, but there was a connection, deep and old, that had stirred inside the man and encouraged him to try again to be a father to his now grown child. And even if his real-life father had disappointed Hideo's fantasies in almost every way, his father had reached out to him and Hideo was hungry enough and open enough to give the man a chance.

As for Hideo's mother, she had been opposed to his plans from the beginning and remained so. But despite her disapproval, Hideo felt that she understood his desires. He had tried to win her over by asking her if it wasn't natural for a boy to want to know his father. And he tried the other card I suggested he play—wasn't it natural for an American-Japanese dual national to want to know his fatherland America? What could his mother say, except to warn him that his father would just disappoint him some day, and that he would find that he was a stranger in America and that Okinawa was his real home? And when Hideo persisted with his plans, she gave him her blessing as graciously as she could, saying "Go ahead and find out for yourself."

He had appeased her by promising to return to Okinawa after finishing community college. Of course, he would not be the first youth to make that kind of promise to his mother and eventually fail to return. But Okinawan youth often return home after adventures in the mainland or America, finding that they miss life in the islands. And it was hard to imagine that Hideo could stay away from his mother for very long. Their bond would not weaken easily and could someday, perhaps sooner than later, bring him back home to his mother's side. One could hope that both he and his mother would grow while they were apart.

But the important thing was that he was taking the challenge. He was acting. Hideo was separating from his mother and going out into the world. He was putting his own needs first and daring to hurt another's feelings. He was starting to grow into the adult that he wanted to become. Hideo was living his life as an adventure.

I was happy for him. Hideo was owning his separateness and assuming responsibility for his life. He was accepting the consequences of his actions and opening himself to the possibility of deep intimate connections with self and others. As he embraced his sensual and emotional intimacies, he discovered the yearnings of his soul, and a song emerged. Hideo had discovered his voice. He was celebrating himself, singing his song. I told him that he was a hero on an adventure. He smiled, and suggested that perhaps that was an exaggeration. But I think he liked this expression, and I meant it, in the sense that when we truly attempt to live, we are living heroically.

He questioned whether he could really change himself.

I warned him, "Well, don't expect too much, you're probably not ever going to be the life of the party."

Hideo smiled, and almost laughed!

"But you have changed already. You are really living now. You will always be shy and quiet, but that doesn't have to stop you. As a shy person you may attempt and do almost anything."

A FINAL HANDSHAKE

Our final hours were devoted to attending to his fears about leaving his mother and his impending departure. Old symptoms reappeared as self-doubts, and he questioned whether he could really pull off such a grand scheme. Could he really leave his mother? Could he really get to know his father? Could he adjust to life in the United States? Staying at home and the gas station suddenly seemed appealing again. He complained that maybe he wasn't ready yet.

I think that his anxiety was also about the end of therapy and partly because he would miss me. After all, he had finally allowed himself to trust someone with his feelings and had benefited from our relationship. Ending also evoked vivid memories of the painful loss of his father and stimulated anxiety over the potential loss of his mother. I tried to assure him that such regression before the end of therapy was common, and warned him that his growth would not be linear because issues are never completely resolved, but recur again, requiring reinforcement of lessons we have once learned.

But I encouraged him that he no longer needed me and that his growth was now a part of him that would go with him wherever he went. He was now able to trust and open himself to his father or others, just as he had done with me. I told him that I had also gotten a great deal from working with him. He seemed surprised, so I tried to explain.

"I learned about your experience, your life, how it's different from and similar to mine. I guess because we are both American and Japanese that talking with you brought up a lot of feelings and memories. And in trying to help you deal with things, I also helped myself at the same time." I then gave him a playful dig: "I also learned to be patient when someone doesn't talk much."

Hideo smiled; he had learned to laugh at himself.

And soon our time was up. Hideo had changed. He had begun to build a life for himself. He had dared to confront his pain and fear. He had wished and enacted his dreams. Yes, he was a hero on an adventure. Perhaps Hideo wouldn't think so, but I wouldn't hesitate to describe him in that light. Although I knew that he would continue to face intense struggles, he had come a long way and I felt happy for him. As he got up to leave our eyes met.

"Well, take care of yourself, I'll miss you." And as I said the words, I choked a little; it was true, I would miss him.

His eyes became teary and he nervously nodded his head up and down. "Thanks" is all that would come out of his mouth, but his eyes expressed his gratitude.

I put out my hand and we shook. His hand was as cold and limp as ever but this time he looked me directly in the eye and gave a genuine smile whose warmth dissipated the chill of his hand. I held onto his hand.

"If you're going to the United States you've got to work on your hand-shake."

Hideo was puzzled.

"Americans like them firm," I said. "Imagine you're squeezing the water out of a hunk of tofu," and I clasped his hand tightly.

Hideo smiled and squeezed back.

CHAPTER 3

The Fruit of Our Own Doing

Freud tells us to blame our parents for all the shortcomings of our life, and Marx tells us to blame the upper class of our society. But the only one to blame is oneself. . . . The problem is not to blame or explain but to handle the life that arises.

(Campbell, 1988, p. 161)

"I don't need counseling. I'm not crazy. It's my professor. He is the one who needs counseling! I am not the one with the problem . . . well, okay, yes, I have a problem—HE is my problem!"

Khermani repeated some variation of this statement every session. And I would think, "Okay, so you want to deny that you need help. You want to blame everything on someone else. You want counseling, but you don't want to admit it. Why can't you accept that this is counseling?"

But then I would ask myself, "Is this really counseling? If the client doesn't acknowledge the therapy, can it really be therapy? If the client says that he doesn't even want to receive therapy, can it be called therapy and can it be therapeutic?"

I have worked with young people from various countries who have taken a similar stance. The stigma against mental illness extended to counseling. It was difficult for them to imagine that they were in any way part of that terribly frightening world of insanity and asylums. For them, mental illness meant being crazy, being taken away, and never returning. For some, it was a label attached to those the government wanted to dispose of—the weak, the elderly, or political opponents.

It was probably hard for Khermani to conceive of talking to someone about his problems as a way of resolving them. This skepticism is understandable. Receiving an interpretation, prescription, and treatment is a shamanic tradition practiced widely in many countries, but consulting with a professional who does not claim the power to heal is a strange experience for most people in the world. It is only natural that they doubt the efficacy of a process that promises only that in lengthy sessions of talking with a trained person, something positive may emerge from the understanding of self and other or from the relationship itself.

Khermani would begin each session with a question about what actions I had taken during the week on his behalf. "So, did you talk to my professor?" "Did you meet with the department head?" "Did you write a letter to the dean?" "Did you arrange for me to meet with the president?"

Sometimes I had done what he had demanded and other times I hadn't, but it didn't seem to make any difference—either way he would be disappointed in the outcome. I would try to discuss the merits and demerits of possible courses of seeking redress, but with a growing feeling that he would sabotage any action that I initiated through his rash actions.

As we talked, Khermani would soon move away from last week's demands to voicing his most recent complaints and describing the latest incidents. He claimed to be often wronged, victimized by others, and he was stridently self-righteous. He was brittle and irritable and often sarcastic and provocative. His focus shifted from one grievance to another. The time passed quickly and he controlled the session with his insistent talking overwhelming my normally laid-back style. Our dialogues seemed to mire in the muck of complaints and accusations.

"Coming to Japan was a big mistake!" he claimed.

"I'm sorry that you feel that way. I wonder what we can do to improve the situation?"

"Get me a new professor!"

"How would you describe the problem with your professor?"

"He is an idiot, he knows nothing!"

I would sometimes try to shift the focus from complaining to considering alternative courses of action.

"Let's consider your options." I suggested. "Would one possibility be going back to Iran?"

"Are you joking? We all want to get out!"

"Well, another option is to stay here. What is positive about being here?"

"I thought I can do research here."

"How is your research going?"

"How can I research in this environment? The program here is terrible!"

He may be right, I thought, but there was little I could do to change the situation. So I tried to explore other areas of his life.

"How is living in Japan in other ways?" I asked.

"Japanese are prejudiced toward foreigners. They look down on Iranians. They think we are all here working as cheap, illegal laborers."

I constantly struggled to move away from such exchanges, which could take up considerable amounts of time unless I aggressively attempted to shift the focus to a more productive tone. I would try to say things like, "So I think I have some understanding now of the problems you are facing. Let's try to focus now on what we might do to address these problems."

And often he would stop himself, and say, "Okay, okay, never mind." But invariably a few minutes later he would begin his tirades again. I knew that the most important thing I could do for him was to maintain our relationship and not allow him to drive me away. I persevered, but I became impatient and felt that I was failing him. He battled with me during the sessions and belittled the importance of my assistance, which was not producing the results he wanted. But there was always a surprise for me as I attempted to end the sessions.

"Okay, you are busy. I am taking too much of your time. So when can I see you again?"

Perhaps my facial expression said to him, "Are you sure you want to come again?" because he would then explain, "I know you can't really help me, but what would I do if I couldn't come here? Where would I go? Who would listen to my problem?"

LOST IN JAPAN: FINDING ONE'S WAY WITHOUT WORDS

As my worries grew that he was right, that I really couldn't do much for him, I greedily grabbed those bits of encouragement. They kept me going and believing in the value of therapy. But I could see little sign of improvement. Khermani remained obsessed with his professor, whom he described as irresponsible, immature, emotionally volatile, prejudiced toward foreigners, and vindictive.

On the other hand, his professor assured me that Khermani was the most difficult student he had ever encountered. He was demanding and obstinate and his professor was becoming worried that Khermani's hostility was endangering the harmony and stability of his research group.

All of Khermani's energy seemed tied up in the relationship with his professor. I tried constantly and futilely to move our attention to Khermani himself. I suggested to him repeatedly that he put some distance between himself and his professor. "I realize you are angry with your professor, but if you could put some of that energy into your research it might progress a lot more."

Khermani would scoff at my comment, dismissing it with a flip of his hand as if to say that I knew nothing of the complexity of his situation. He was convinced that his problems with his professor were much greater than I, or anyone else, could imagine.

I began to see that Khermani was waging a battle to maintain his dignity in the face of extreme adversity. He had come from Iran at 27 with a history of excellent academic achievement. He had received a degree from a top university, worked for a while in a good job, and been selected to receive a scholarship to study at one of Japan's best universities.

However, life in Japan had never been quite as Khermani had imagined, and he soon ran into trouble. Told that Japanese was unnecessary since he could study in English, he had come without any knowledge of the language. But it was more necessary for his daily life than he had thought. He found his communication limited, and social contacts with Japanese people few. Although he had studied English he was far from fluent, as he had never been outside of Iran before. He found his English limited in expression, and his understanding incomplete. He avoided Japanese students because of his poor Japanese skills, but also shunned social contacts with other foreigners fearing that they would impede his Japanese progress.

Khermani also distanced himself from other Muslim students. He did not take part in the Friday prayer on campus and seemed uninvolved in Muslim activities. I knew that Muslim students exhibit a wide range of responses in their understanding of what constitutes the essentials of Islam and Islamic law and what is required to be a good and responsible Muslim. For many who are in their first experience of living outside their home country, questions and conflicts emerge about their religion, and I wondered what Islam meant in Khermani's life.

The first signs of difficulties were in Japanese language class where he was noticeably uninvolved. He was frequently absent, often late, and inattentive or uncooperative when he came. He appeared angry or agitated and isolated from other students. His teachers began to worry about him as he appeared preoccupied and made little progress.

Khermani began to go to his science lab, but reports came that he was quarreling with others there. He refused to speak Japanese and demanded that they speak English. A classmate came by to say that Khermani was behaving erratically and dangerously in the lab and had told him he was having a hard time sleeping. He was talking negatively about his research and relations with others. His professor called to say that he was worried and had recommended that Khermani go to the hospital for a check-up, but Khermani had just laughed at him.

It was around that time that Khermani had first visited my office. I invited him in and he sat down heavily, looking haggard and anxious. He spoke quickly and with some tension, and made fleeting eye contact.

Khermani did not then, or ever, ask for therapy to help improve his mental condition. Instead he asked only that I do something to help to correct the conditions in his lab. His professor, he complained, did not do his job. He did not provide adequate supervision and he failed to support Khermani's research. His professor was not a bad person, he said, merely a fool.

He had numerous stories of how he had been wronged, but the most striking and confusing was one about his father's death.

"My professor wouldn't let me go home when my father died," he claimed in an angry voice. "I couldn't go to my father's funeral!"

How terrible, I thought.

But "Not so," claimed the professor when I questioned him. And he told a far different and stranger story. Khermani hadn't even known of his father's death until nearly 6 months after he died. His mother had come to Japan specifically to break the news to him. I wondered why, until an anthropologist colleague whom I consulted explained that it was common practice in Iran. It is considered inappropriate to inform a child of the death of a parent by telephone or letter, and so the news may be kept hidden until the opportunity comes to inform the child face-to-face.

I wondered how common this practice is today, but I did hear the story of an Iranian student who in a similar situation became extremely distraught when a fellow Iranian expressed condolences about her father's death. The student was shocked and disbelieving, as she had heard nothing from her family.

While I took this knowledge in intellectually, I found it strange and upsetting. My experience in working with people who were grieving the deaths of loved ones had led me to believe in the importance of going through a mourning process. An essential part of this grief work was to come together with others who shared the sorrow. Depriving a child of the opportunity to grieve his father's death with his other family members was incomprehensible to me. But I knew that I had to regard my own belief as culturally determined in the same way that Khermani's family's beliefs were.

So while it was hard for me to accept what had happened as an appropriate way of dealing with loss, I could now understand why Khermani had not been able to attend his father's funeral or even known about his father's death. But I still didn't understand why he had blamed his professor for the situation. Was it just part of his way of blaming everything that went wrong on one person?

The relationship with his professor had not always been bad. In fact, Khermani admitted that his professor had been very kind at first. He had invited Khermani to his house for dinner and had been helpful in his research. But then the renowned professor had become busy and had asked Khermani to consult not with him, but with the associate professor. Did Khermani feel abandoned? Khermani refused to listen to the advice of the associate professor, saying that he would take directions only from the professor. Actually, he was the same age as the associate and felt that in terms of knowledge and experience he was superior. Khermani's actual position in the lab's hierarchy, however, was at the bottom. Was his pride hurt to have to consult with someone whom he regarded as his inferior, yet was clearly above him in the university hierarchy?

An article I found informed me that Iranians rely on a social code that prescribes correct behavioral patterns toward those in each position in a hierarchy. People in lower ranks respond to those in higher ranks with deference, politeness, and respect even though they may feel resentment and hostility toward them. This cultural form was supposedly instilled by authoritarian regimes demanding submission and respect of subjects, but can also be observed in the father-son relationship. Khermani's behavior, however, was clearly out of line with this cultural pattern. His resistance was no longer held in check but was running rampant over his acceptance of authority.

As with any graduate student, the heart of the matter, of course, was Khermani's research. If he achieved results, I thought that he could overcome problems in human relations. But I also knew that in Japan, if not elsewhere, human relations overrode objective measures of achievement. If a person was considered to be one of the group members, then he would be protected regardless of his performance. And if someone was not part of the group he could be scapegoated and sacrificed. Khermani was already isolated as the only foreigner in his lab, and his troublesome behavior had surely placed him in a precarious position.

His professor insisted that Khermani did not work productively, while Khermani claimed that he had achieved sufficient research results. Khermani cried that his professor was prejudiced so could not judge his work. When I asked a third party for an objective evaluation, I was told that Khermani's research was inadequate, but I doubted that one professor could openly contradict another in a Japanese university.

FACING THE ANGER: MAINTAINING CONTACT

As weeks went by, Khermani began to complain that since I was not able to help him, he would have to take his case to those with more authority. He vowed to take his case to the department chairman, the president of the university, or even to the prime minister. He wanted me to call in the press, embassy officials, or anyone else who would listen and take action. Khermani said that he knew many other foreign students with similar problems. The problem was not his personally, but a problem with the university and perhaps all Japanese universities, and maybe Japan itself.

I knew that he was right, for I had heard similar stories from other international students. But I also thought it highly unlikely that the entire fault lay in the system. Students like Khermani can cause a great deal of trouble for a professor, making unrealistic demands on their time. Their inability to communicate easily verbally and to understand nonverbal communication can create numerous misunderstandings and conflicts.

Khermani was a big man with a sharp glare and a loud voice and a swagger in his walk that intimidated others. I heard that he had once thrown a book through a window in anger. But a psychologist friend who had worked in Iran cautioned me that Iranians were emotionally expressive people who showed tears, affection, and anger easily. They tend to indulge in a lot of verbal exaggeration, he claimed. So was Khermani's threat just an expression of this cultural pattern of behavior? Was Khermani aggressive and dangerous or just being "Iranian"? Placed in the context of Japanese society, where cultural norms generally prescribe control and reserve in emotional expression, the behavior of someone like Khermani can become distorted and seem extreme. After all, he had never actually touched anyone in the lab.

Sometimes in the sessions he would become agitated and threaten that he was going to get violent with his professor, knock him down and kick his head. However, if I pressed him, he would soon reassure me that he wouldn't really do anything. His professor, though, seemed worried about the possibility of being attacked, and the possibility of sabotage, such as through the destruction of equipment or data. I too feared the possibility of Khermani's sinking into feelings of hopelessness that could lead to either a suicidal attempt to escape the torment or a violent attack against one of his imagined tormentors.

Even as I considered such an outburst of violence unlikely, I had to admit that Khermani's anger scared me. I am uncomfortable with a person whose anger seethes out from him and suddenly and unexpectedly erupts, disrupting the niceties of social customs and formalities. But I knew that it was important to allow him the space to express those feelings and to legitimize them. I needed to stay with him, despite my discomfort. I tried to reflect his feelings.

"You seem angry about the way you feel you are being treated."

I tried to empathize with his feelings.

"I think I can understand how you would be angry about what happened."

I tried to help him to express his anger in more productive ways.

"I realize you are angry, but is there a way of expressing your anger that still enables the other person to respond and actually encourages dialogue?"

"Like what?" Khermani asked.

"I mean without accusing, without blaming the other person . . . talking in a way that leaves room for the other person to stay with you rather than run away?"

"I don't know what you mean."

"Let me give you an example. You could say, 'I am upset that you did not read my paper and I would like to know why.' That would make it easier for your professor to respond to you than saying, 'You are a bad professor and do not give me good supervision.'"

These interventions all seemed to have some positive effect in the therapy, but I felt that I needed to deal with Khermani's anger more directly by focusing on the immediate situation in the therapy room.

So I got up my courage to ask him, "Are you angry with me too?"

Khermani seemed surprised by my question, and looked at me more directly.

"Why should I be angry with you?"

"I don't know . . . maybe for not helping to solve your problem . . . for not believing your explanation . . . for not taking your side."

At first Khermani denied his anger, "No, it's not your fault. You are not able to help, that's all."

"But if you were angry at me, I could understand it. I really haven't been able to help you in the ways that you have asked me to."

This time Khermani shot back, "Why didn't you tell the chairman that my professor was harassing me?"

"I didn't do it because I didn't think that he would believe me, and I thought it might do you more harm than good to tell the chairman. He would certainly tell the professor, who would in turn get angrier."

"Okay, okay, maybe you're right. But sometimes I wonder whose side you are on."

"I want to help you. I want to help your professor too, but he has plenty of people to help him. I want to help the two of you to get along well enough so that you can get your research done and get your degree. . . . So, I'm sorry that I'm not able to achieve the results you would like."

This exchange seemed to open the door to more direct expression of feelings in our relationship. I felt that I allowed him to be angry at me. I hoped that he would learn to express his anger in a more constructive way. In any case, I felt more able to maintain contact with him, and not abandon him.

A PARANOID NARRATIVE? IN THE BORDERLAND OF ANXIETY AND PSYCHOSIS

My most pressing concern was that Khermani's thoughts often seemed paranoid and even delusional. He perceived himself to be the victim of a conspiracy by his professor and others. He could not understand their motives. Although he could rationally and logically explain the basis for his beliefs, he was unable to consider alternative evidence or explanations.

But was Khermani really paranoid? Vigilance is required in assessing paranoia in minorities. They may often have valid reasons for their complaints that others are biased toward them or treat them unfairly. They can have good reason to suspect that others are against them. Therefore their accusations of prejudice and discrimination must be treated seriously because they are commonly experienced by vulnerable minorities, such as foreign students.

General attitudes of Japanese toward Iranians were certainly negative. Some Japanese claimed to be afraid of the Iranian men who congregated in city parks on Sundays. They were welcomed by the small businesses that needed unskilled labor, but ambivalently by everyone else, including a Japanese government afraid of allowing foreigners into the country. Some Iranians told me that they prefer to call themselves "Persian," partly as a way of attempting to escape from the negative stereotypes to which they felt subjected.

So if Khermani felt that others looked at him with critical and fearful eyes, he was probably right, at least some of time. And if he felt vulnerable, well, foreign students have a vulnerability that other students do not. They are temporary guests, as the Immigration Bureau reminds them, and many are receiving scholarships directly from the Japanese government. They fear that if they step out of line they may be sent back home, dashing their dreams of educational advancement.

My reading of Iranian history and culture warned me that Iranians have learned to live with uncertainty, distrust, and cynicism from a long history of adaptation to adverse political circumstances. An Iranian psychiatrist advised me that this may be manifest as a sense of mistrust in interpersonal relationships in which individuals feel that they must always be on guard to protect themselves, fearing that others will take advantage of their trust. I wondered how to utilize this generalized cultural knowledge.

I imagined that living in an environment in which a person cannot understand much of what is going on around him or her would aggravate a sense of mistrust. Should I assess Khermani's mistrust as less extreme than I suspected because his cultural background inclined him to be mistrusting? On the other hand, I was also aware that he was far more distrustful than the few other Iranian students I knew.

He had been to a neurologist, who had prescribed some tranquilizers, which Khermani had taken for a few weeks. But he didn't like the side-effects and had stopped taking them when he ran out. I recommended that he go back to the hospital but my suggestion fell on deaf ears.

I wondered how his symptoms had developed. The precipitant of a distancing by his professor was perhaps in itself insignificant, but may have represented the loss of a sustaining and supportive figure. Were old memories of childhood miseries revived and rage from old frustrations unleashed? Freud claimed that the onset of paranoid thought occurs with a disappointment of love or a social relation leading to a wave of libido that finds no outlet and sweeps back regressively to the point of fixation in a noisy attempt to recover lost love. An unconscious layer of misery and suffering is covered with a conscious layer of organized and vindictive activity.

As with many foreign students, Khermani's lack of understanding of the words and behaviors of the natives confused him and fed his growing sense of paranoia. He was aurally impaired, socially isolated, and lonely—all important factors that can lead to altered perceptions. He had built a delusional story of some plausibility that accounted for his suffering and explained incomprehensible experiences. This explanation offered relief from confusion and the relief in turn worked against abandonment of the explanation.

Khermani directed his attention to small details, challenged me repeatedly, showed irritability at my interruptions, and took inordinate measures to set the record straight. He would come to the sessions with a notebook in which he kept records of all communications between himself and his professor. He occasionally insisted that what I said be written down and signed. He provided copies of everything for me so that I too maintained a thick folder on his case.

His defensiveness and suspiciousness turned former friends into persecutors. His feelings of being taken advantage of heightened the inflexibility of his demands and his tendency to blame others. He appeared neither to examine his beliefs skeptically nor to allow me to challenge their validity.

After considering the possibility that the alleged discrimination was real and weighing the consideration of general cultural patterns and norms, I still faced the question of just how paranoid he was. Although Khermani's grievances seemed excessive, even delusional at times, at other times his grievances appeared justified.

Khermani seemed to be in a strange state in which the distinction between normal and abnormal was unclear. Without hallucinations and a clear psychosis, Khermani was able to function in daily life. He often appeared quite within the range of normality. He was able to think clearly and was obviously oriented in regard to time and place. His behavioral and emotional responses to his beliefs appeared to be appropriate and his thoughts well systematized and logically developed. He was strikingly intact, and showed no evidence of difficulty in perception, clarity of thinking, or affect.

But when Khermani repeatedly voiced the same complaints with new supporting evidence, and calls from his professor kept coming complaining of new incidents, I began to despair. And I had to acknowledge that ominous signs were increasing in our relationship. I feared it was losing its human quality of relating as friends or allies. I questioned whether Khermani was crossing that critical boundary that separates the troubled, suffering, anxious person from the psychotic.

I looked for clues in how I was treating him. Wasn't I beginning to objectify him? Khermani was in danger of no longer being a person to me, but instead a delusion, a DSM psychiatric diagnosis. I was finding it difficult to work with him, to feel his presence and engagement in the therapy process. I worried that the relationship between us was full of concealment. Worst of all, I was even wishing that he would get worse so there would be no question of the psychosis and his need for medication.

Some psychiatrists maintain that psychosis can be diagnosed by the character of the therapy relationship. The patient should be considered psychotic if the therapist no longer has any sense that he or she and the patient are allies who are working together to improve the patient's mental health. I wondered if I still believed in the prospect of his development or if I had given up on that possibility and instead only hoped to keep him out of the hospital and prevent him from destroying himself.

I decided that I needed to intensify my efforts to get him to go to a psychiatrist for a consultation. As always, I approached him gingerly with my request. At first, he eyed me strangely and then with a turn of his head away from me and a flip of his hand dismissed my suggestion as unnecessary. But I knew that I had to persist, for my sake as well as his.

"You think I am crazy?" Khermani laughed nervously.

"I am just saying that you are clearly upset about what is happening and it wouldn't hurt to be more relaxed. Your thoughts also seem confused and if you could get a little clearer you might be able to do your research better."

"No, it will not help," Khermani said, closing the door on the discussion.

In desperation I tried another approach. I contacted a senior Iranian medical doctor who was doing research at the university and explained the situation, taking care to protect Khermani's privacy. He offered to talk directly with Khermani. So after I got Khermani's permission, the three of us met in my office. After we engaged in some small talk, they conversed in Farsi as I sat and observed, not understanding a word.

Finally, they turned to me and with a smile the doctor assured me, "Khermani will go to the hospital. He has promised me that he will go."

And he did.

MEDIATING AND NEGOTIATING;
CULTURAL PATTERNS OF BEHAVIOR

So Khermani went and came back triumphant. He said that the psychiatrist told him he was normal. Later I received a call from the psychiatrist, who said that while Khermani's thoughts seemed a little paranoid and possibly delusional, antipsychotic medication did not seem necessary. Compliance would also be a problem, he felt. Anyway, he didn't think it would work unless Khermani was more anxious and agitated. So he advised me to bring him in again if his condition worsened.

I was surprised because psychiatrists in Japan usually dish out drugs freely. One reason is because that is what most have been trained to do, rather than psychotherapy. Another is that the health insurance system reimburses them by the drugs they give, the tests they order, and the number of patients they see. I felt grateful that this psychiatrist had exercised restraint in prescribing antipsychotic medication.

But now I was stuck with Khermani. I couldn't send him to a hospital. I couldn't even get a psychiatrist to declare him psychotically delusional and prescribe medication. He was my responsibility. Just as I had expected, I had no choice but to continue to try to work with him in therapy.

As Khermani's persecutory way of thinking was unlikely to change quickly, I tried to control environmental stressors. Since he was extremely isolated where he lived, I helped him to move closer to the city. Recognizing the limits of what could be done in one hour a week of counseling, I tried to locate and enlist the support of concerned others, especially fellow countrymen and other Muslim students.

I also worked to get him a new advising professor.

"Impossible," I was told by the authorities. I questioned why.

"Departmental rules prohibit changing advising professors."

"But doesn't it make sense to permit changing when it is in the best interests of the student and the department?" I asked naively.

"Perhaps," admitted the official, "but that's the rule."

But was there another reason? Was there a cultural explanation? A Japanese colleague told me that the reason was simply that Japanese are extremely concerned with loss of face. Changing advising professors did not just mean a change of research interest or acknowledgment of a poor match, but was regarded as a sign of failure by the professor to convince the student of his authority, a sign of being rejected by the student, a sign of inadequate knowledge.

His explanation seemed convincing. But complex cultural analysis often disguises more simple political and economic motivations. Could it be a matter of power? The more students, the more power? Or could it even be a matter as crass as money? The more students, the more research funds?

I pushed a little harder on the issue, because I know that in Japan there are always so-called *tatemae*, meaning rules or public statements that are covering the surface of a more complicated *honne*, or reality. If careful attention is paid to honoring these *tatemae*, exceptions can be made. So if Khermani remained with his present advising professor on paper, he would be free physically to move somewhere else. The difficulty then became finding someone who would take in a student recognized as "a problem." Renegade professors do exist—mostly young men who have spent many years in the United States and reject the traditional ways of doing things. However, no one would take Khermani.

I questioned the position I was taking. As an insider to the university system, what could I do? Should I encourage Khermani to adjust to Japanese culture, assuring him that his professor's behavior, while inadequate, was standard practice in Japan? I knew that if he were accused, other professors would feel obliged to defend their colleague. While I thought that the professor should do more for the student, I felt powerless to take on him and the whole university system. And even if I did, any long-term effect of my efforts was not likely to help Khermani in his attempt to complete his doctorate.

But in seeing myself as part of the system, wasn't I dismissing my own minority position in the university and those of others who shared my position? I felt affinity with Khermani as someone often treated as an outsider. I had drawn the wrath of his professor by suggesting that he apologize to Khermani for his inability to properly supervise him as a gesture of regret and reconciliation. "Do you really understand this university?" he challenged me. I was obviously seen as not Japanese, a foreigner, an outsider. I identified with Khermani's feelings of vulnerability and isolation as one regarded as a stranger. I wanted to advocate for his rights as a student. I wanted to change the system, for myself as well as for him.

I seemed to be placed in a mediator's role, between Khermani and his professor. My reading on Iranian culture had informed me that when conflict develops in Iran in families and among friends, mediators are extremely important in reconciling the two parties by facilitating compromise and allowing each to save face by not giving in. Was Khermani expecting me to fulfill this role?

I brought them together on several occasions, hoping to decrease conflict between them, including those disputes over who was responsible for the problem. I attempted to externalize the problem by posing it as one of mutual interest—how to help Khermani graduate. I tried to help them to move away from the sense of failure that had developed in response to the continuing existence of the problem. However, the meetings degenerated into each blaming the other. In the end, they were unable to cooperate and unite in a struggle against the problem.

I had a growing feeling that neither changing the system nor mediation was going to work. My impression was that Khermani was unproductive in his research, and I imagined that this reality was deeply disturbing to him and connected to his problems. I was sure that he suffered from feelings of inadequacy. As a proud and elite academic, he could not accept that he was failing. Again I wondered how much to consider culture, having read that Iranians are very proud, and therefore boastful and impatient with learning, and have difficulty admitting mistakes.

I considered the applicability of acculturation theory, which would label Khermani as adopting a marginal style of adaptation. He would be described as open to his own culture, yet closed to the host culture. I knew that like many other foreign students he worried about his family back home, missed his supportive network of trusted friends, and had great difficulty in making new friendships with Japanese. He appeared to resist becoming acculturated and felt alienated from his surroundings, wallowing in the anxiety of the present and the uncertain future. Yet I heard claims that Iran has managed to absorb cultural influences without losing identity and continuity, and wondered if Khermani could do the same in Japan. Was it possible to help him by changing his mode of acculturation to one that is considered healthier, by enhancing his openness to the host culture? I tried to encourage him to reflect on how to adapt better to Japanese culture.

"You know, if you could apologize to your professor for what you said, I'm sure things would improve."

"I should apologize to him?" he responded incredulously. "After all that he has done, why should I apologize to him?"

"I realize that you feel he has done you many wrongs, but you are also telling me that you accept that you too did not act properly on occasion. You told me that sometimes you spoke disrespectfully. If you could apologize for your own behavior, it could allow him to apologize for his behavior."

"No way. I will never say '*Sumimasen*' like Japanese always do. They are always saying '*Sumimasen, sumimasen*.'"

"You know, in Japanese, '*sumimasen*' doesn't mean 'It was my fault.' It just means that you feel bad or at least recognize that a problem has occurred. It doesn't mean that you apologize and take blame or responsibility for what happened. Saying *sumimasen* is simply a gesture of humility and desire to smooth relations. By lowering your head, you encourage the other person to lower his too. So it's a way of avoiding confrontation and conflict.

"It may be different in Iran," I continued, "but this is a culture steeped with rituals and customs of apology. If you want to survive here, you have to perform these rituals. If you try to use the same values and rules that are accepted in Iran, it just won't work here."

Khermani was unmoved by my explanation, and only convinced that my suggestion indicated that I did not understand the situation at all.

"It is impossible."

"But if you could do it, it could improve the situation. Why can't you do it?"

Khermani smiled at me as if to say, I can see you are trying to help, but your attempts are futile.

EMPATHIZING WITH THE HURT AND LOSS

Therapy continued weekly with a modest goal of stabilizing Khermani's mental condition rather than of completely eliminating his paranoid style of thinking. I wanted to avoid a disaster that would ruin his health and damage his career. However, I was worried that I was colluding with his expectations that nothing would happen in therapy, or if it did, that it would come from me.

I encouraged him to take better care of his health, to eat better, exercise a little, and get more sleep. We talked about the meaning of religion in his life and I suggested he attend the Friday prayer of the Muslim students. My feeling was that participation in religious ritual could have a positive effect on Khermani's mental health. Besides bringing some discipline to his life, there was also the possibility of receiving the benefits of social support and friendship from his involvement.

Whenever possible, I attempted not to get too involved in the details of his numerous grievances and not to validate them. I tried not to become preoccupied with the details of his system of paranoid thinking.

However, I did empathize with Khermani's difficult position and feelings of confusion and hurt, and of being victimized. I wanted to recognize and respond to his feelings of loss and frustration.

Introducing new ways of viewing things continued to be difficult. It seemed that in Khermani's paranoid world what is new was not permitted and not plotted into experience. Instead, all was assimilated into pre-existing forms, everything confirming the already established singular and tragic plot. All other ways of interpreting experience disappeared. The possibility of a future did not seem to exist. Life was a self-fulfilling prophecy in which Khermani first expected an event to occur, then acted in a way to bring it about, and finally relegated awareness of his behavior to the unconscious. His paranoid stories were unlike cultural narratives in which people must mediate between good and evil both in themselves and in the world. Instead his stories consisted only of his own struggles against evil.

As his therapist I wanted to be someone with whom he could test these paranoid narratives. I continually encouraged him to allow a new explanation, a new view. I asked him to consider that the struggle of good and evil was within each of us. And I invited him to let me enter his aloneness, to engage with me and recreate himself. I believed that he was separated from others because he was separated from himself. By recognizing his strangeness, he would suffer from it less, and he would learn to accept others by realizing his own disturbing otherness.

But therapy was blocked by his failure to assume responsibility for creating his own life predicament. For Khermani the extraordinarily difficult step of acceptance of responsibility constituted the major therapeutic task. Although he always appeared on time for every appointment, he would never follow the suggestions I made to him for during the week. In other words, he could not find the time to help himself, but he would never miss a chance to ask me to help him.

Khermani displaced responsibility to other individuals and forces. He disowned and attributed to others his own feelings and desires and invariably explained his problems and failures as a result of external influence. He was the innocent victim of events he himself often unwittingly set into motion. Despite my best efforts, he denied any personal contribution to his unhappy situation. He could agree on an intellectual level that if he just finished his work there would be no problem, but found a thousand excuses not to. Ultimately I would have to help him assume responsibility, but how?

ACCEPTING RESPONSIBILITY IN THE HERE AND NOW

I believed that real therapy would begin only when Khermani was able to accept authorship of his projected feelings. But he could not face his own personal responsibility for his life and process of change. If he was responsible, then his time in Japan had been a failure. He had wasted 3 years of his life and faced returning home a failure.

I attempted to move away from a focus on providing simplistic solutions for him. This obviously was unproductive. Instead, I tried to focus on the process of how he related to others.

One day Khermani produced a letter from his professor, and pointed to a line that had particularly enraged him.

"Look what he wrote! He said that he will not talk with me any more!"

I read the note and disagreed, "No, I don't think so. 'I cannot talk with him' means that he finds you difficult to talk with."

"No, he said that he will not advise me any more," he insisted.

We went back and forth till finally I said, "Okay, let's try to look at this objectively. You have good English, but are you a native speaker of English?"

He looked at me skeptically.

I repeated my question, "Are you a native speaker of English?"

"Okay, no."

"Am I a native speaker of English?"

"Yes, of course," he admitted.

"And do I have a doctorate from Harvard University, a university that you respect?"

Khermani nodded.

"And would you agree that my understanding of English is greater than yours?"

"Maybe, in general," he grudgingly admitted, making me want to lean over and shake him and say "Come on, damn it, admit that my English is better!"

But I controlled my impulse and said, "So would you agree with my interpretation that your professor did not mean that he will not talk with you any more, but only meant that he finds you difficult to talk with?"

Khermani would not back down. He insisted, "No, he meant that he is not willing to talk with me any more."

I took a deep breath and settled back in my chair, moving away from Khermani. He was driving me crazy. In my feelings of frustration I wanted to rub the evidence in his face. Even when he was obviously wrong he wouldn't admit it. What could I do, I wondered, to help him to admit that he was wrong? He easily dismissed my comments when we worked with second-hand material for which his defenses had already been constructed.

I tried to focus on the immediate situation of what actually transpired in the therapy situation. I believed that an awareness of my own feelings was my most important instrument for identifying how he contributed to his own predicament.

I turned our attention to us. What was the outstanding feature of our relationship, I asked myself. Frustration? Boredom? Irritation? Yes, I was frustrated and I was irritated. I was also bored with his repetitive complaints and denials. I needed to confront him in some acceptable way. He could deny responsibility for everything else, but not for what he did to me.

"I am feeling very frustrated." I said to him.

I imagined that Khermani looked at me with more interest.

"I am very frustrated and irritated with the way you are talking with me right now."

"Why?" asked Khermani, seeming to really want to know.

"Because you refuse to acknowledge even the most obvious reality. I feel that you are not listening to me. I also feel that you do not trust me, even in such an obvious case when I am right and you are wrong. I feel that I can never help you or satisfy you."

Khermani was uncharacteristically quiet. So I continued.

"I see you doing this with me here and I believe that what happens here is important because it gives a clue to some of the problems that exist between you and others. If you talk in this way with your professors, I think that they will feel the same way I do. I think they will get frustrated and irritated. And then they will stop listening and the chance for communication will be lost."

We sat in silence for a while, until Khermani finally said, "Okay, so maybe you are right this time."

I hoped that getting Khermani to focus on his existence in the here and now would set him on the path toward accepting responsibility. As he became aware of how he relates to his own self, it would encourage honesty and genuineness. I believed that he would be more legitimate with self and others, and begin to recognize and be responsive to the norms and taboos of his social and cultural groups.

I repeated this kind of statement several times in different sessions, whenever the opportunity arose. I hoped that he would learn how others view his behavior, and how it makes others feel. He might also get some sense of how his behaviors create the views others have of him, and in turn influence his own self-image.

But I had a heavy feeling, as if I had all the responsibility for making something happen. Khermani just didn't seem capable of assuming any responsibility for changing his situation. I assumed that a familiar cultural metaphor might be more powerful for him, but unfortunately I was too ignorant of his culture to provide any.

I had read about *taghdir*, described as a deep-rooted Iranian cultural belief in fate. It reminded me of the Japanese concept of *shikata ga nai*, as both involve an expectation of accepting the outcomes of life with grace. *Taghdir* seemed to mean that those who showed strength in submitting to the authority of someone like a professor would be accorded respect. But Iranian students whom I questioned told me that this attitude has decreased visibly among the educated, who are more likely to believe that it is up to the individual to change his or her life. Like many aspects of traditional culture anywhere, for some people it may influence their lives mostly as an internal or intergenerational conflict between expectations and desires. I asked Khermani how he felt about *taghdir*.

"That is an old belief. Young people don't think like that any more."

"So you yourself don't believe in it?"

"No."

"Would you say that you believe in the importance of the individual in changing his life?"

"Yes."

"So, how would you like to change your life today?"

Khermani seemed to ponder my question heavily but could not answer.

AWAKENING TO BITTERSWEET DISCOVERIES

Just as I was feeling that our time together would never be therapy, just maintenance, Khermani broke the dam with a surprising confession. One day as we settled into an exhausted moment of silence after another outburst, Khermani looked at me with a strangely sad expression and said, "I may be very skillful with computers, but I'm not very skillful with humans."

I was stunned. This was the breakthrough I had been waiting for. He slowly began to talk more about himself and reflect on his actions. Now that he had bared himself, I wanted to gently help him face the issues, detail by detail, until the misery was unveiled. In this way, I believed that the intensity of his paranoid concerns would gradually fade.

However, I sensed that Khermani feared this awakening. There was too much regret, too much loss, and he resisted opening up too much, too soon. He returned again and again to his complaints.

Despite his awakening, Khermani continued to find it difficult to identify his responsibility in the life of the problem. But he was disconcerted to discover the extent of the problem's influence in his life. I reached for questions to inspire him to investigate what these new developments in awareness might reflect about personal and relationship attributes and qualities.

I asked him in what way his discoveries might affect his attitude toward himself. I encouraged him to think about what difference it would make about how he feels about himself if he acted on these ideas. We considered what he might find easier to do in his life. Of course, we reflected on how these insights might affect his relationship with his professor, and we faced the difficult question of what he might be able to do now to salvage his life.

Once he assumed responsibility, therapeutic change seemed to transpire naturally. He moved from projecting his failures to making excuses for them. Then he began to feel anxious about them. I took these as signs of growing strength. However, as he faced details of his failure in life and as he realized the damage he had inflicted on his life, he became disheartened.

I felt that even this depression could be useful because it implied recognition and acceptance of responsibility for self-inflicted failure, a momentous step for someone accustomed to using denial, projection, and contradiction. I wanted to help him welcome his sadness and feelings of responsibility for what he had done, believing that this would help him to grow. We worked on mending the fences he had torn down. We saw what could be done to reestablish ties that had been severed and to recognize what could not be renewed.

As space emerged in our meetings, we also discussed Khermani's religious beliefs. He felt torn between adherence to Islam and a desire to fit in and be liberated from constricting practices and beliefs. Ambivalence about consuming pork and alcohol was symbolic of deeper conflicts regarding sex, family, responsibilities, career ambitions, and a sense of personal identity. As he wrestled with these conflicts, Khermani became more regular in his prayers and felt that Islam offered him the chance for corrective repentance for his guilt-inducing sinful acts.

Khermani also spoke of his relationship with his father. He felt dominated by a father who at the same time encouraged him to take more responsibility. Khermani felt burdened by heavy expectations of taking on his father's role as head of family. As the eldest son he should become the patriarch of the extended family. Issues of submission and competition with his father clearly related to his problems with authority figures.

Finally our time ran out, along with Khermani's scholarship. In the end this was the best we could do. We had achieved some acceptance of responsibility, some insight, less blaming of others, and some efforts to rebuild his tattered life. We began to face his departure. I encouraged him to make plans for the next step in his life. He would return home for a while, he decided, and apply for a fellowship to study in the United States.

I wondered how he felt about leaving me. After all, he had faithfully visited my office once a week for nearly 2 years. He had opened up to me more than perhaps anyone else in his life. I sensed his yearning for closeness and dread of loss. Perhaps it was a sign of his fear of autonomy or softening ego boundaries, but Khermani developed a fascination with psychology. He talked of changing his field and becoming a psychologist and asked if he could become my student. When I was less than enthusiastic, he asked for introductions to psychology professors in the United States. I tried to steer his energy into reflecting on and attending to his new awareness of interpersonal weaknesses and resolve to change this aspect of himself. I supported his newfound curiosity about his inner life, if not his career change.

Until his final days in Japan, Khermani continued to ask what I could do to help him graduate. But I knew that the time had long since passed when he could do much more to rectify his situation.

"Prepare yourself for your journey," I admonished him.

When he stood outside my door at the end of his last visit, he thanked me again for my help. I felt grateful for his words. As he began to walk away, he asked once again, "So is there anything else I can do?"

"I think you have done all you can," I answered.

He shrugged his shoulders, let out a huge sigh, gave me a weary smile and walked away.

As I watched his retreating figure, I reflected on our work. Certainly no miracles had been performed. I hadn't even helped him to obtain his degree. Had I done only damage control? Khermani left Japan without his doctorate, but also without a record of mental illness or of expulsion from the university.

Perhaps Khermani never expected concrete results from me. But I imagined that deep inside he hoped that I could help him somehow to deal with the fears he was confronting. He sought some brief refuge from the frustrations and terror of his lonely position. Although he could only occasionally articulate this need, his few revelations of vulnerability were extremely poignant.

Was Khermani a casualty of overseas study? Certainly his defenses had been overwhelmed by his experience of living in a foreign country. Although he no doubt had struggled with similar issues at home, he probably never would have confronted such formidable circumstances as he had encountered in Japan. Perhaps the United States would have been easier.

His challenge had shaken him to the very core of his being and threatened to destroy the world he had constructed. But his crisis had also brought an opportunity. Khermani may have failed in his self-assigned task of acquiring a Ph.D., while succeeding in the unexpected but ultimately more critical challenge of becoming more human.

CHAPTER 4

The Power in a Name

Human existence cannot be silent, nor can it be nourished by false words, but only by true words, with which we transform the world. To exist humanly is to name the world, to change it. Once named, the world in its turn reappears to the namers as a problem and requires of them a new naming.

(Freire, 2000, p. 75)

When she first came to my office, Hiromi explained that she was thinking about dropping out of school. Her studies were no longer interesting and she was thinking that maybe she should quit and start working. She was also tired of living at home, she said, and wanted to become independent of her parents.

Hiromi had been a student of mine the previous semester—and a very memorable one. When I introduced the topic of Koreans in Japan, Hiromi had spoken up with assertion and a conviction uncharacteristic of most of the Japanese students I had known. From the emotional tone in her voice I had sensed that she was close to the issue. She had also utilized a journal that I required for the class to express herself further, and it was there that I discovered that Hiromi was of Korean ancestry.

I wondered what, if anything, being Korean had to do with her present predicament. Since she had written often of her identity conflicts, I assumed that they were part of the picture. But since she was saying that her problem was deciding whether to quit school, we began there. Although the issue usually comes up eventually, in my experience very few people come to counseling with a presenting problem of ethnic identity confusion or conflict. Perhaps people regard it as too insignificant a problem to warrant the attention of a professional consultation, so they wrap it in a more socially acceptable package, such as the issue of withdrawal from the university.

So we explored her feelings about her studies. Hiromi realized that she had been attracted to American education because it offered an opportunity to explore areas that she had never been exposed to in Japan. She had first thought of studying computers, but became drawn to sociology and psychology. In her classes the treatment of topics of prejudice and discrimination were especially stimulating, and teachers were eager to learn from her about the situation in Japan. At first she had been embarrassed by how little she knew, but she used term papers as an opportunity to research about Koreans in Japan for the first time in her life. She felt supported by her professors and the minority students in her classes and was enthusiastic in her searching.

She had felt such excitement and filled her journal with expressions of profound discovery. As she positioned herself as part of an oppressed minority, her life took on new meaning. As her understanding increased of the marginalizing social pressures that produce and maintain minorities as disadvantaged, she felt a building indignation. Her feelings of shame and reticence were transformed into intense pride and assertiveness.

But Hiromi had also written in her journal about great confusion. Her awakening had brought realization of not only what she had gained, but also what she had lost. Joys of finding herself were accompanied by despair over lost years of living as though half asleep.

Hiromi complained that she had grown weary of her studies. The thrill was gone. Her desire to become a sociologist was fading rapidly with nothing emerging in its place. So what had happened? What had caused her to lose her spark? How had her motivation vanished, how was her purpose lost?

I told her that she had made a great impression on me as a student. Her ability to speak out articulately in class about an obviously emotional topic was admirable. I also said that her willingness to wrestle with deep issues and to openly share them in her journal had made me hope that she would continue to pursue these forms of study and self-expression.

As we explored her disillusionment, she began to talk about being Korean. She said that she had become tired of thinking about it. Her courses had been great at first and she had felt liberated to deal with such personal issues in her studies, but she had started to feel burdened by the subject.

"I started to feel like I didn't want it to always be on my mind. I just felt tired of it all. I was spending all this time thinking about it, but I realized, what difference does it make, I mean, who cares if I am Korean? Does it really matter?"

"But at first it was very meaningful to you. Do you know what happened to change that?" I asked.

Hiromi became silent. I grew impatient waiting for her to answer, but told myself to slow down and give her time. I reminded myself that Hiromi had never been in counseling; this was a completely new experience for her. I glanced at the clock, looked out the window, and took a deep breath to try to rid myself of the tension that sprang from my need to be doing something to fill the space.

I recalled a study I had conducted in which students in Japan told me that they thought it was okay to wait even up to 3 minutes to answer a teacher's question. They expected the teacher to wait while they discussed the question with classmates. I realized that my expectations of immediate answers were from another cultural context.

After what seemed like minutes, but may have been no more than 15 seconds, Hiromi spoke. "I spent my whole life trying not to think about it. I mean I always knew I was Korean, but felt the message from everyone that it was something to forget about, to just bury."

When I asked her to explain more, she continued, "When I started to think about all these things, I realized that I have spent my life as a phony. I appear to be Japanese on the outside, but inside I am Korean. I don't tell this to anyone, and I pretend to be Japanese instead. But after coming to this American university, I started to wonder what was going on. Why was I living a double life?"

She looked at me with what I thought was an accusing manner. "Your class really upset me." I felt defensive, but she quickly added, "but in a good way, I suppose. The video you showed of the Korean high school girl really shocked me. I couldn't believe that would be a topic in a university class."

In her psychology class I had introduced the standard topic of identity with a video of a high school girl who decides that she wants to reveal her previously hidden Korean ancestry. She announces that she wants to now be known by her original family name and so publicly identified as Korean. At the time I imagined only that I was broaching a subject that other students could benefit from being exposed to. I didn't know that there were Korean students in the class or how they would react.

"I thought she was so brave and I was such a coward," Hiromi said. "I started to hate myself. I felt uncomfortable with other people, because I kept thinking, if I was honest I would tell them I am Korean. I felt constricted, like I was suffocating in my relationships with Japanese. That's when I started to think about quitting school.

"My boyfriend was Japanese, maybe you remember him 'cause I wrote about him in my journal. I started to feel strange about him. I wondered why he wanted to be with me. Was there some reason that he wanted a Korean girlfriend? He always claimed it didn't matter to him what I was. But I suspected that it did, because he said once that his parents wouldn't mind if we wanted to get married, since I was a Japanese citizen. Did that mean that if I were not naturalized they would reject me? Why did my legal status make me acceptable as a daughter-in-law? Did it transform me in some miraculous way from a Korean to a Japanese?"

REEVALUATING A WORN-OUT NARRATIVE

I wondered why the class had been so disturbing to Hiromi. As she explained more about her life, a clearer picture emerged. Hiromi's ethnic self-narrative had portrayed her as a well-adjusted person to whom ethnicity was not an important part of her identity. She had reasoned that she was far more Japanese than Korean and therefore not to tell others that she was Korean was not really being dishonest. Hiromi had denied the existence of prejudice and discrimination in society and even blamed ethnic troubles on "nationalistic Koreans."

But Hiromi's confrontation with certain realities forced her to face more complex and problematic issues. In the class we had discussed the problems that plagued Koreans in Japan and the dangerous trap of blaming the victim. Her denial began to loosen and disturbing thoughts appeared. She began to find that her self-narrative was no longer useful in defending her way of seeing and living in the world. With my encouragement and support, she began to reexamine her life narrative and reflect on the past.

"The article you gave out on Korean identity really shocked me too," Hiromi told me. "You know the one where at the beginning a girl talks about a scene from her childhood when she is walking down the street with her friends and she notices her grandmother coming toward them. I couldn't believe it when I read it; it was like I was reading my own story because the exact same thing happened to me. But somehow I had forgotten about it for a long time. Remembering it really bothered me."

"I didn't realize that you were upset by that story," I told her.

It was silent again, but I felt more comfortable this time just sitting there with her. Hiromi looked down for a while before speaking.

"I was still really young, around second grade. I was with my friends from school and we were walking home, talking and laughing. I looked up and there was my grandmother coming toward us. I felt faint as though I was trapped in a sinking, awful feeling. I dreaded what would happen if she saw me and waved or called my name. Then everyone would know I was Korean.

"You see, I was hiding it from everyone. I never invited anyone to my home. Even if they saw my parents no one would know, but my grandmother was different. To me, she looked Korean. Or maybe it was her smell. The rest of us were careful not to eat too much *kim chee*, but grandmother had to have it every day and I was sure that the Japanese could smell the garlic from her body.

"When I saw her coming I felt panicky. If she spoke to me it would blow my whole cover; all would be lost. I looked for an escape, but there were no side streets, just walls of houses on either side. I put my head down, but my friend said something to me, and when I didn't answer, she kept asking me what's the matter? As my grandmother neared us, I put my hand up in front of my face to hide even more. After a while, I looked up but would not turn around. My friends were making fun of me for acting weird. I felt sick to my stomach and ran home."

Hiromi looked away and said, "I loved my grandmother more than anyone. I wondered if she recognized me and knew what I was doing, but she never said anything about it."

Despite Hiromi's distress, I was not completely there with her. I was recalling the shame I had felt as a child in the United States when I denied knowing my mother's Japanese name when asked by some curious inquisitors. I was sure they would make fun of it, pronounce it funny and laugh. They were incredulous when I claimed that I didn't know her name. They insisted that I must know. "What does your father call her?" they asked. Again I tried to evade them, "He just says 'Hey you.'" They laughed and let me off the hook. But I was not so kind to myself; the experience lingered with me. When we were taught in Catholic school about the sin of Peter when he repeatedly denied knowing Jesus, I felt that surely I was as bad and pitiful as Peter.

I attempted to reengage with Hiromi. I wanted to comfort her but didn't know how. I felt that at least I could show her that I understood the pain in such formative experiences. "I know that those early experiences can really hurt. It's hard when you feel embarrassed by your own family and deny them. But it's not easy for a kid to face prejudice."

I decided to go a little further. "Something like that happened to me when I was a child and I've never forgotten it either. It stays with you."

Hiromi looked at me with a new expression of recognition and I felt that we were more together than before our mutual revelations.

This was one of the experiences that Hiromi had to integrate into her evolving sense of self. It was no longer enough to say simply that she was really Japanese since she had Japanese friends, ate Japanese food, went to Japanese school, lived in Japanese society, and spoke the Japanese language. Questions burned in her mind. Didn't experiences like the one with her grandmother make her a little different from Japanese people? But what could she say was Korean about her? Did eating kim chee make her Korean? Or was it just the blood that mattered?

I wondered how Hiromi had made sense of such experiences as a child. Did she just feel different, outside, like she didn't really belong? Did they make her feel self-hatred? Did she wish that she were not Korean? Or did she identify with being Korean as a way of preserving her self-dignity?

I assumed that like all children, Hiromi had felt an intense need to be like others. To be different can be a painful experience. I remember the awful feeling of the first day of elementary school. It was bad enough to anticipate being stared at and called a Jap, but I even became filled with dread when I realized that the colored counting sticks that I had brought with me were a different shape from those of everyone else.

It is natural for children to be embarrassed about their differences and to try to negate or deny that which distinguishes them. For Hiromi it meant internalizing mainstream standards and rejecting being Korean. This insidious process is unnoticed by the child, because oppressive reality tends to absorb those within it and acts to submerge one's consciousness. Yet Hiromi's identity was probably shaped by her acceptance of the stereotypes the dominant group holds of Koreans. As a child she would have lacked knowledge on which to base more liberating images. The price can be alienation from a true self. But is there really a true self? In Hiromi's case was being Korean her true self or just a past connection?

Is it right to assume that a true self is always an ethnic self and that all else is phony? Is biology the determining factor in creation of a cultural self? While we deny scientific validity of race, do we persist in believing that something genetic remains the overriding factor in forming an authentic self?

Hiromi began to recall other disturbing but revealing memories. Some of these she related in a journal she was keeping as part of the therapy.

"I was asked a few times if I was Korean, but I just smiled and evaded the question. If people said anything bad about Koreans, I was quiet, so they wouldn't suspect me. Some friends in high school may have known. I told some close friends and they didn't seem to care.

"But for some reason when I was in high school, some Korean youth group members came to talk with me. I told them I wasn't interested in their group. They accused me of being ashamed of being Korean. I blamed them for trying to separate themselves and acting different. They were the ones keeping prejudice alive, I charged. They angrily said I was hiding in an illusion, that I wanted to be Japanese, but I could never be Japanese, because whether I liked it or not I was Korean! I walked away from them. I thought they were crazy.

"Now I don't know. Was I really ashamed of being Korean? Did I really wish that I was Japanese?"

Hiromi's identity as Japanese had always seemed so natural, but now she was recounting examples of being deeply affected by prejudice. She recalled times when she actively rejected being Korean and faced the challenge of incorporating these experiences and awareness into her self-narrative. Hiromi became intensely involved in trying to integrate these previously disavowed experiences of shame, fear, ambivalence, ambiguity, and conflict. She recognized how she had internalized a negative image of being Korean that had been presented to her by majority Japanese.

Although Hiromi may have denied having had traumatic experiences, she was remembering the fear of suffering discrimination if her Japanese friends and colleagues found out about her secret. Hiromi had never wanted to confront the problem that she had known such fear; that she had felt the contemptuous gaze of others; that she had experienced identity conflicts. She had not wanted to realize that she had been scarred by the prejudice around her and the conflicts within her family.

She had always known that however much she had become Japanese, she was still different in some ways from her Japanese friends; her family was different, her experiences were different, and she wondered if perhaps even her ways of thinking and feeling were different. She questioned if these differences were important, or any more significant than those between two Japanese.

IS THERE A RIGHT NAME?

One day, without mentioning it in her counseling session, Hiromi surprised me by signing her journal with the name Hiromi Lee. On the class list her name was Hiromi Nakamura. I assumed that Lee was her Korean family name. From my work with American minorities, I knew that names, both individual and group, can be an important source of concern. I was finding out that the same was true of persons of Korean ancestry in Japan.

Persons of Korean ancestry in Japan have been deeply divided by nationality. Because Japan's nationality law is based on the principle of *jus sanguinis*, it is acquired naturally—basically through registration by a Japanese parent. Those born to parents who are not Japanese citizens become foreign nationals. Koreans have therefore had a choice of becoming Japanese through naturalization or remaining Korean nationals. This issue has acutely separated those of Korean ancestry. Those who naturalize are denounced by those who don't. Those who don't naturalize are further divided by those who are affiliated with North Korea and those who maintain ties to South Korea, although recently this division is becoming less antagonistic along with the reconciliation movement in those countries.

Much of this tension is revealed in personal choices about names. Those who naturalize have either freely chosen, been persuaded, or been coerced into adopting a "Japanese-like" name as part of the ritual of becoming a citizen. Most of those who have maintained Korean nationality have chosen the path of maintaining an official alias that they use in their social life. These aliases are commonly used names in Japan that allow the person to pass as mainstream Japanese. But there is another group of persons who insist on going through life with their Korean names.

Hiromi's family was one of those who chose to naturalize. Her father had explained to her that it made much more sense to become a citizen of the country where they lived and would always live than to remain a citizen of a country they could never call home. They might never be really Japanese, but at least they could say Japan was their home. And they would be less vulnerable to discrimination if they were citizens.

Hiromi had been persuaded by his argument, but was learning that many young people of Korean ancestry no longer believe that an alias is necessary to avoid discrimination. She noticed more people emerging in various fields with recognizably ethnic names. I told her that naturalizers are no longer subjected to forced assimilation policy and that Japanese citizens with names like "Lee" or "Kimu (Kim)" or "Howaito (White)" are reconstructing the definition of what constitutes a Japanese or a Japanese name.

Hiromi began to confront various conflicts. Sometimes she felt angry and blamed Japanese people for her problems. "Because of their racism I have had to suffer. Why do they think they are better than Koreans?"

At other times she said that she felt guilty that she wanted to continue to be invisible. She questioned if she should go through life as she had, hiding her background. Or should she be defiant and change her name as a way of protesting discrimination? But on the other hand, was she really Korean? Even her parents were born in Japan. She didn't speak Korean, couldn't write it, and didn't know much about Korea. How could she claim to be Korean? If she learned some folk songs or dances and put on ethnic dress would that make her Korean?

And if she did change her name, what would happen? Would old friends abandon her, and new ones avoid her? Would potential lovers evaporate and possible jobs disappear?

She knew that if people wanted to find out her roots they could investigate her family register, which would reveal all. The suicide of Arai Shoko, a nationally prominent politician of Korean ancestry, shook Hiromi. Like her, he was a naturalized Japanese, and she wondered if it was her fate, too, to be encumbered and tortured by her roots forever.

As a way of helping her to deal with her struggles, I introduced Hiromi to a group I had met who were dealing with this very issue. They were actively pursuing the "return of their ethnic names" in the courts. All members were the offspring of naturalizers who had done as they were told by authorities and surrendered their Korean family names and adopted more Japanese names. Now adults, these individuals were asserting their right to live as Japanese citizens who publicly acknowledge being of a different ethnic background from the majority. Their actions were a direct challenge to the state ideology of a monoethnic nation and a myth that all Japanese citizens come from the same ethnic background.

I personally detest this ideology and have devoted part of my professional and personal life to challenging it. But I became disturbed that perhaps I was following my own needs, rather than Hiromi's. I questioned whether I was perceptively following her lead by proposing that she attend the meetings of this group or introducing my own agenda. How much was I pushing her? Did I worry that Hiromi was resisting my efforts to change her?

No doubt influenced by this group, Hiromi began to assert that living under a Korean name is tough but living under an alias is tougher. When I asked her why, she said, "It's easier to bear the difficulty of presenting yourself honestly. By using an alias you are silently agreeing that being Korean is bad so it must be hidden. It's better to be honest and open by revealing all and confronting reality together with the Japanese."

I struggled to understand the realities of her situation as a young Korean-ancestry person better. Through my study, I realized that the situation has changed immensely over the years, and that much conventional knowledge was no longer true. While Hiromi's Korean grandparents were forced to change their name, her parents were only pressured into using a Japanese alias. For their generations, it was a common understanding that prejudice in Japanese society made it impossible to use a Korean name without suffering discrimination. But Hiromi's generation increasingly uses Japanese-like names as much out of a sense of familiarity as necessity. Many claim to no longer feel inhibited by the threat of discrimination.

As I explored more on the topic of names, I began to understand that it was not simply a matter of Korean name or Japanese name. People had come up with various creative means of constructing names. Some used a Korean reading of their name. Others took a common Japanese name and wrote it in Chinese characters Korean style. There is a great variety of individual expressions revealed in names, each an attempt to name one's world and to transform it.

OUT OF TUNE? APPLYING AMERICAN THEORIES IN JAPAN

Hiromi was clearly moving in the direction that I had hoped. Her journal entries were now signed by her complete Korean name, Young Mi Lee.

I told her, "There is a Native American saying that 'a man's life proceeds from his name in the way that a river proceeds from its source.'"

Hiromi smiled so I decided to say more.

"I went through something similar to what you are going through when I was a student. I changed my name to reveal my background."

She gazed at me intensely and asked, "Are you glad you did it?"

"Yes, it was very important for me at the time."

Hiromi seemed lost in thought for a moment, then said, "I feel very different to say Young Mi Lee than Hiromi Nakamura. It helps me to feel more Korean. It expresses who I really am."

Therapy was moving along nicely, I thought. She was not just reflecting, but also engaging in action—naming her world and changing it. But still I questioned my approach. Were my standards too American and naïve and inappropriate in Japan? Was I assuming that asserting a Japanese identity in the United States, as I had done, was equivalent to asserting a Korean identity in Japan? Wasn't I mostly ignorant of the social realities of being Korean in Japan? Was I too involved in an image of myself as a liberator of oppressed Japanese minority youth? Did I take myself too seriously as a role model?

In other words, how much was my self-narrative influencing therapy? I believed that no one should hide their family origins. My awareness of the importance of names to minorities had come not only from my encounters with others, but from personal experience. I felt that I had boldly asserted my ethnicity when I was younger by changing my name to reveal my ethnic origins at all times, should anyone care to know. Did I therefore feel that Hiromi should do the same?

Actually, to be honest, her identity struggles were more disturbing to me than that. Now that I had entered middle age, my identity problems were something that I wanted to put into the past. I was embarrassed to be reminded of the tormenting and consuming conflicts I had experienced, and the way I had publicly announced my crisis through several name changes in my student years. I had been comforted somewhat when I learned that even some of the most famous psychologists, such as Harry Stack Sullivan and the founder of the concept of identity himself, Erik Erikson, had done the same. But as I moved away from the self-absorbed stage of my life into engagement with my new family and career, I began to trivialize identity problems even as I taught about their importance and counseled youth who were going through them.

With Hiromi I wanted to be supportive, but I also felt an impatience, a desire to push her away from what I sometimes felt were frivolous concerns. I recalled a poem that my father, perplexed by my suffering, had written to me in the midst of my identity crisis:

A peach hanging on a branch
Wonders is it an apple or a plum?
No it is a peach hanging on a branch

Rather than being amused, I was annoyed by his silly poem. What did he know about identity? He was White! Actually I hardly thought of him as White, as he was the son of Irish immigrants, although he himself never gave a damn about his roots.

It is strange how we change, because now I felt like reciting that silly poem to Hiromi as she sat there wallowing in what I thought was a problem of her own making. Perhaps I should recite Shakespeare: "What's in a name? That which we call a rose by any other name would smell as sweet." Was a name really so important? Is it true, as a Japanese proverb says, "The name reveals the person?"

I was forced to reflect on my years of identity conflict and reembrace the agony—legitimize the struggle. Despite whatever embarrassment I suffered in revealing my identity conflicts, I believed strongly in what I was doing. And still do.

These reflections helped me to keep focused on distinguishing my issues from hers. Because of the experiences I had had, I hoped to help her find similarly satisfying, if different, approaches to her problems. I acknowledged that I needed to learn from Hiromi about her own realities, rather than impose my incomplete understanding on her situation. I also wanted Hiromi to do what my father had always encouraged me to do—to maintain a sense of levity, to have some humor and at the same time take things seriously, and to see the absurd as well as the solemn—not an easy thing to do.

FACING FURTHER COMPLEXITIES OF IDENTITY

Then just as I thought I was understanding her, Hiromi shocked me one day with what appeared to her to be a casual revelation. "I'm not close to my mother's parents, maybe because they were against her marriage with my father," she disclosed. When I asked why, she replied, "Because my mother's family is Japanese."

I was stunned. I couldn't believe that Hiromi had never mentioned it before. I blamed my relaxed approach to history taking. I wondered how she could think that it was unimportant.

So Hiromi's mother was Japanese! And more important, Hiromi herself was Japanese! Her mother had been disowned and cut off from her family after marrying a Korean. So Hiromi had grown up deprived of her Japanese family.

Again, I had to deal with my own identity. Mixed ethnic identity was my professional specialty. I had turned my own identity struggles into a clinical and research career that continued long after my dissertation on that topic was completed. I wondered how she could treat being mixed as such an unimportant detail of her life. And I questioned how much I resented her denial of being mixed, when for me it was such an assumed area of similarity that should be mutually acknowledged.

Here too I had to confront my American expectations. The multiracial movement in the United States was in full force and previously denied multiple identities were being asserted. But there were few signs of activity in Japan, where social custom still dictated that if you were part Korean, you were Korean and not Japanese. Hiromi had not felt the space to assert more complex and multiple identities. This is despite the fact that while the existence of discrimination in marriage continues, the vast majority of Koreans today marry Japanese, not Koreans. The mixed Korean-Japanese population may number nearly half a million, yet discussion of their existence is rare.

When I expressed my surprise that she had not told me earlier about her mother, Hiromi seemed equally perplexed that to her I was making a big deal out of it. "It didn't seem important to mention," she said.

But I persisted, "We are talking about your identity, and the fact that your mother is Japanese is not important?" I asked incredulously. Hiromi defended herself well. Her mother always talked negatively about Japanese, as though she herself was not Japanese either, she explained. By marrying a Korean, she had left the Japanese and entered the Korean community. I wondered about the hardship her mother had endured. These were certainly social realities that I needed to understand.

But Hiromi also began to reflect on her lack of attention to her Japanese ancestry. "Perhaps it was just too complicated. Just being Korean is difficult enough." And she faced some painful memories. "My Japanese grandparents never really accepted us. They never completely rejected us, but when we were together with our full Japanese cousins, we could feel the difference in the way they treated us. . . . But our Korean grandparents also sometimes said hurtful things about us."

Being of mixed ancestry was something that Hiromi began to deal with in her journal. "I remember once my Korean grandmother said when I did something she didn't like, she said to me, 'You are bad because you are Japanese.'"

Hiromi was reading some writing by Japanese-Koreans who referred to themselves as "double" as a way of accepting both parts of their background. She returned to signing her name Hiromi Lee, perhaps a sign of her acceptance of a mixed identity. "The two always seemed so antagonistic to me. I always felt, if you were Korean, then how could you be Japanese? But I know that both are a part of me."

I told her, "That is something that I have learned too. It can be hard to hold on to both—to claim to be both. But that's mostly because others can't see you in that way. They want it black or white. Or in Japan, they want you to be Korean or Japanese, American or Japanese. It just makes it easier for them. When you insist that you are both, it creates incredible confusion and discomfort for other people."

"Yeah," Hiromi answered. "I noticed that people really don't know how to treat us. If they find out I am Korean then they see me as Korean. But if I tell them my mother is Japanese, then they feel uncomfortable to just call me Korean. And if I insist that I am Japanese I can tell that they can't really think of me as Japanese since I am part Korean."

"So where does that leave you?" I asked

"I guess I just have to figure it out for myself—what it means to be mixed, both. And decide whom to tell and when and how much about myself. Everyone doesn't need to know everything."

I wanted to share my experience with her. "You know I have thought a lot about this myself. It still continues today. I think you have to choose your battles carefully. Otherwise, you will get tired of fighting. When it's inconsequential, it may be better to just go for simplicity, just tell people whatever is easier. But when it's important sometimes you have to assert yourself."

"Yeah, I don't think I can go around telling everyone I'm both Korean and Japanese. Japanese people just don't know what that means."

The timing seemed right so I returned to an old theme. "You once asked if perhaps you didn't wish that you were Japanese, when the Korean students questioned you. But you *were* Japanese, not just because of your mother but also because of the way you grew up."

I realized that this was something that I could not have said years earlier when my thinking was more rigid about ethnicity. In the past, I would have felt that she needed to identify more as Korean and not as Japanese. I was learning that the accentuation of a minority self was not necessarily more authentic than the expression of other possible selves for any individual.

INTEGRATING NARRATIVES:
ENGAGING IN SELF-DEFINITION

Around this time the school year was ending and I was leaving for a trip abroad. Hiromi had decided to return to school in the fall full time and appeared to be doing well. She was still using Lee as a name, saying that going by a Japanese name was no way to live. "It's just an escape, not a solution to the social problem," she said. "That way we lose the opportunity of allowing Japanese to face the situation too."

I thought counseling was very successful. Identity conflicts had been confronted. Hiromi had embraced and integrated her secret background and emerged with an assertive identity as Korean. She had been able to acknowledge the importance of being mixed, as well.

But when the fall semester began, I was surprised to find the name Hiromi Nakamura on a class list. Wasn't that her former name that she had officially changed in the spring? When I called off the names in class she raised her hand for Hiromi Nakamura, but I still assumed that it was a clerical mistake that would be corrected.

Hiromi came to see me and explained that a lot had happened during summer vacation. She had recognized some conflicting truths and complex realities.

"In the United States, to Americans, I am Japanese. It doesn't make sense to claim to be Korean. In the eyes of others in daily social life in Japan too, you are Japanese. In the minds of others who know your background you are Korean. In your own mind you are both and other things as well," she explained.

When I asked about her name, she said, "I realized that it is only natural to live with the name you have used your whole life. My parents don't like getting mail addressed to me in my Korean name. They have worked hard to maintain secrecy and they feel that my actions jeopardize their safety. And my parents would never address me by my Korean name.

"Besides," she continued, "the days are gone when we had to work in restaurants or game parlors. Japanese society has changed. If we have the ability, we can get jobs anywhere. Success depends on the individual. Now we young Koreans can do anything we want," Hiromi asserted.

"Fighting discrimination every day through my name is just not necessary. My political awareness has grown, but my Korean name just doesn't feel familiar . . . like it's somebody else, not me. Maybe I am afraid of discrimination, that's true, but the more important reason is I just want to live naturally. It is convenient and familiar to use a Japanese name; it doesn't mean anything.

"Of course, if anyone needs to know, I will tell them without hesitation that I am Korean, but I know that there is a lot more to me. I am also Japanese, and a lot of other things as well. I am really both—both Korean and Japanese. I know that Korea is not my homeland; maybe Japan isn't either, but it is more than Korea. Now that I am more strongly Korean, or

I mean, feel more confidence, I don't need to use a Korean name. I can't limit myself just to Korean friends. Nationality doesn't matter. What matters is how an individual thinks and acts in life."

Hiromi was just reporting to me; therapy had clearly ended. We talked of how much she had changed since we had first met. Then I wished her well. She thanked me and said, "See you in class."

At first I felt like therapy had failed. My own involvement in issues of personal and social change and a philosophical stance of therapy as liberation inspired me to want to encourage Hiromi in certain directions. And I had to admit that I was disappointed by her eventual choice.

But why should I feel defeated? Hiromi had come a long way. I had to accept that it was perhaps the best choice for her. My awareness of the important therapeutic function of revealing secrets about one's identity motivated me to encourage honesty and self-revelation as more positive than assimilation achieved through disguising one's background. But still I knew that such encouragement must be done with an awareness of the social situation that clients face. In a society like Japan in which being different and being Korean are reasons for exclusion, coming "out of the closet" is greatly feared. The degree to which an individual's decision involves one's whole family also makes decisions about revelations of ethnic secrets an extremely heavy burden.

Taking seriously my role as a reflexive participant in therapy meant learning to care less about such issues as whether Hiromi changed her name and more about supporting the movement she initiated. I was reminded that identity resolutions are very individualistic; we are not all required to aggressively assert our ethnic background as the main aspect of our identity.

I learned to question more deeply my assumptions that the ethnic aspect of an individual was somehow more important and authentic than anything else. Hiromi was teaching me that this belief is just another form of the essentialism on which discrimination is based. Is adopting a Korean name to recover a Korean identity necessarily the right thing to do for all Korean Japanese? Or for some people, is it a denial of the Japanese aspects that they have acquired through socialization in Japanese society? Must a Korean Japanese forever be Korean to be authentic?

After all, I told myself, I can't possibly know what is right for her. What I had done in my own life was in another place, in another time. And what of my own children, who unlike their father live very much like Hiromi, their Irish American ancestry not revealed in their name or face? How could I know what is best for them? It was after all my decision to have them go through their childhood with a completely Japanese-like name.

Why? To avoid unnecessary alienation. But like Hiromi, their challenge becomes to maintain a positive connection with a hidden background. This is usually easier if that part is American rather than Korean, but perhaps like Hiromi they too will decide that life is easier when you can appear to be an ordinary Japanese and determine yourself to whom and when to reveal your other selves.

CHAPTER 5

The Colors of Blood

Daring, if you will, to contemplate, to question the underpinnings of a society in which I am counted among the sleeping unbeautiful. But who, one fitful night, discovered that for years, centuries even, she lay dreaming in a land that had fallen into a deeper sleep.

(Wilson, 1994b, p. 59)

We all have skeletons in our closets. But for some people these skeletons are not remnants of their own actions but are ghosts of the ancient past. They are not the shadows of individual sin but of stigma assigned by others. The phantoms are passed along from one generation to the next, surviving along with the social attitudes and beliefs that created them and keep them alive. And sometimes we don't even know that the skeletons are there until we open the door one day and discover them hanging there.

In our very first session, Ayako told me the story of the discovery of her family secret. "When I was 14 I was at home one day alone. There was an opened letter from the city hall on the table. I looked at it and realized it was a copy of my family register. I had heard about them but had never seen one, so I opened it and read it. I noticed the names of my father and my mother, their marriage, and my name at the bottom as the oldest daughter. Then I read through the notes and noticed that my father had once changed his permanent address. The old address seemed strangely familiar and I suddenly realized that it was in a part of the city where *burakumin* live. I just kept staring at the address."

I knew very little about *burakumin*, except that they were people with some connection to an outcaste group in feudal times and that this connection was shrouded in secrecy. My ignorance is not unusual in Japan. Although there are a few million people who might be designated *burakumin*, public knowledge is extremely limited and discussion of the issue muted by an unspoken taboo. Those who do speak out have often been silenced by those who attempt to control the words and images portrayed in the media. All Japanese know a little about *burakumin* but few people talk openly and it is rare that people tell you they are *burakumin*.

Since they tell no one about their ancestors, and appear no different from majority Japanese, they are largely invisible. The document Ayako had discovered, the *koseki* (family register), is the way that *burakumin* origins can be traced. In this system of social control, all citizens are registered in a document that contains numerous details about family members and their origins, including permanent address, previous permanent addresses, former nationalities, adoption, illegitimacy, and so on. Since certain areas are recognized as *burakumin* communities, a permanent address can identify an individual as *burakumin*.

"What were your feelings and thoughts?" I asked her.

"I just couldn't believe it. It was like a wave of heat swept through my body and flooded my head. I can still remember it. I was numb and felt dizzy, like I had to sit down. I just couldn't believe that my father was from a discriminated hamlet. Because that meant that he was *burakumin*. And if he was *burakumin*, that meant that I was part *burakumin*! I felt like I was in shock. After a while I put the letter back into the envelope and shuffled slowly to my room. I lay down on the floor and just stared at the ceiling. I don't remember that part. It was like I was in a daze. I guess several hours passed, because I heard my mother come home.

"After a while I got up and waited till she was sitting down at the kitchen table sipping tea before I approached her and blurted out, 'Mom, I saw the *koseki* and dad's old address. Does that mean daddy is a *burakumin*?' She looked at me strangely and said 'Yes.' 'And so am I half *burakumin*?' I asked her. My mother shook her head, 'No, she said, you are all *burakumin*; I am also from that *buraku*.'

"I couldn't believe it. I said to her, 'Why didn't you ever tell me?' She just said, 'I always assumed you knew.'"

"How did you feel about your mother at that moment?"

"I don't know, I was a little confused, but mad too. I felt like maybe she had tricked me, by not telling me. But I don't know if I really wanted to be told."

"So that was the great awakening?"

"Yes, I guess you could call it that."

Until then Ayako had gone through her life aware that *burakumin* existed but never imagining that she herself was considered to belong to that group. Her father had moved from the old address before she was born and had moved his permanent address to the present one. When he married, his wife was moved from her parents' register to his. But the family register still recorded the father's old address as well. Ayako had never had a reason to look at her family register before and so the family roots remained unknown to her, and no one had mentioned it either.

But what had she discovered? The knowledge that she was considered to be a member of the group who were descendants of people designated as social outcastes in ancient times mostly because of their occupations dealing with the flesh of animals or dead humans and religious prohibitions against such "unclean" activities. There is also the theory that they were discriminated against because they came from Korea, although in actuality early settlers from Korea were aristocrats revered by the Japanese. Later outcastes were officially designated by the Tokugawa government as a special segregated class at the bottom of society. The Meiji government put an end to this caste system that placed samurai at the top and abolished discrimination in 1871, about the same time as the abolition of slavery in the United States. Since then their special status has survived only through the determined efforts of individuals to maintain class distinctions with an emperor at the top and others at the bottom, and by linking descendants to their ancestors and discriminating against them.

Ayako explained, "At my high school we had special *burakumin* education, and so I learned about the history of discrimination and how people were treated as animals rather than human beings. Because they did special jobs like with leather or handling dead bodies they were segregated and discriminated against. Even today some people still think there is something polluted about *burakumin* and try to avoid them in marriage or even in hiring employees."

"How did you react to that education?"

"It was strange to hear all that. Because I hadn't grown up thinking there was anything wrong with me. So I kept wondering, are they talking about me? It didn't seem real at all. I mean, it seemed like something so removed from my life and I couldn't really relate to it at all. It didn't seem to represent my life."

That was 5 years ago, and Ayako had pushed thoughts of her background aside until she had come to a branch campus of an American university in Tokyo. Far from her hometown, she probably would have continued to ignore this issue for several years, but for her encounter with the subject of *burakumin* in her college courses. Unlike at a Japanese university where the topic is taboo, at her American university professors considered the subject an interesting and relevant illustration of prejudice and discrimination for sociology or psychology classes. For Ayako it was an unexpected opportunity to explore the meaning of her background. Despite my limited knowledge of *burakumin*, I was one of those professors who raised the issue in my classes. But I had never actually met a person who admitted to being *burakumin*, and wondered how helpful I could be to her.

PURE, MIXED, BLUE, GREEN:
CONFRONTING THE POLITICS OF BLOOD

Ayako was clearly struggling with understanding the meaning in her life of these roots. "I have lived my whole life without ever having received any prejudice or discrimination. I don't know anything about what the *burakumin* experience is. No one has ever treated me badly . . . that's because they don't know."

I asked her, "Do you wonder about that . . . how would they treat you if they knew?"

"Yes, but I think I shouldn't care. In my life people don't really treat me badly. Others may experience bad treatment but I don't. But I also don't feel like it should be a secret. What difference does it make? If people don't want to be my friend because I am *burakumin*, then maybe I don't need them as friends anyway."

"That's one way of looking at it," I agreed. "Anyone who would think badly about you because of your roots would not be the kind of person you would want for a friend. But is it something that is so important about you that you want to let everyone know it?"

"Maybe not."

"What does it mean to you?"

"That I'm different."

"In what way?"

"I don't know."

"I mean are you really different from other people?"

"I guess not."

"I mean is your blood green?" I joked.

Ayako laughed. She had a good sense of humor and I wanted her to maintain some levity about her crisis, and see the incredible absurdity of her situation in Japan.

But I sensed that the reference to blood had made us both uneasy. Blood is a powerful metaphor in the Japanese imagination. In the process of creating a mythology of the nation, Japanese have been transformed into a people who have evolved from a single ethnic source. Japanese blood is supposedly pure, while the blood of certain others is not. Foreigners, of course, lack Japanese blood, and *burakumin's* blood was considered polluted.

The mention of blood also brought out a disturbing reality for me. What color was my own blood? It was my Japanese and Irish "mixed blood" that was salient and made me marginal in Japan—labeled and treated like a stranger, an outsider. It was my fate to be considered different. I later thought this experience helped me to empathize with the struggles of the oppressed.

But the color of my Japanese "blue blood" had been driven into me since childhood in America. When I had first been able to cry and admit to my father that kids had been bullying me for being Japanese, he had told me the stories of my samurai background. He no doubt hoped to empower me to resist my tormentors' attempts to degrade me by instilling in me a pride that I had come from noble roots. And I had delighted in my grandmother's tales of my great-grandfather, a high-ranking samurai. No reason to feel ashamed, they said, you are high class, you are better than they are. And so I was a prince in disguise! How many of my snotty-nosed Italian and Irish tormentors could say that?

I had always felt secure in my minority identity, and my ability to empathize with the oppressed. But I was forced to face the question of how my own attempts at achieving dignity and self-respect had rested on affiliations with the elite background of my ancestors. Did I still feel the need to counter the look in people's eyes that said that a mixed-blood kid born during the Occupation must be the son of a lower-class woman, and probably was illegitimate? Of course I could show off my Tokyo University professorship or my Harvard education as signs of my worth, but my real source of pride was not worldly achievement but a more basic biological claim of blood—samurai blood.

But I had to reflect on difficult questions: How had my self-narrative inadvertently prejudiced me toward others like Ayako? How could I guide her toward self-respect? Could our backgrounds possibly be considered as equally valid and rich sources of dignity? My ancestors had been at the top of society, hers at the bottom. I needed to find the answers—to join her in a search for understanding. And so we began.

ASSISTING THE SEARCH FOR ROOTS AND COMMUNITY

Ayako admitted one day, "I don't even know what else to say, except that I am *burakumin*. I don't really know anything about it."

So I suggested, "Maybe that's a first step then, learning what you can about it. If you want I can recommend some places to begin. There are organizations where you could go and meet people who are involved in *burakumin* human rights issues. I could also introduce you to a friend who has been involved for years in *burakumin* issues. You could even do the investigation as the theme of your term paper for your sociology course. I think it could help you to learn more about what it means to be *burakumin* before you decide if you want to tell people about your background."

"I don't know. I'm afraid that if other students see me studying about this that they may suspect I am *burakumin*."

"You don't have to decide now, just think about it."

It didn't take long before Ayako told me, "I think it makes sense to learn more about my background. I think I would like to do that."

In my work with Ayako I was relying on my experience working with individuals of various ethnic backgrounds in the United States while trying to be aware of important aspects of the Japanese social system that might affect my approach. Although I was dealing with a Japanese situation, I soon realized that there were similar experiences of clients who were passing as something and hiding something else. How many White people are denying and running from a Black past of African ancestors? How many are trying to hide a dark relative in their closet? Or, how many Black people are rejecting their White past of European ancestors?

I thought that ethnic identity models that were popular in the United States would help me in my work with Ayako, but soon realized that there was a crucial difference. Those models are designed for a context in which the individual and others are aware of one's minority status, particularly during childhood. In this case, neither Ayako nor others had known about her background while she was growing up. It had only come to her attention 5 years earlier, and had remained as her secret since then.

She had grown up with a self-image as a majority person, but now she was being challenged to integrate the negative associations with being *burakumin* into the construction of a new identity. Derogatory images had to be challenged. I recognized the importance of accurate knowledge for her empowerment so I encouraged her to find out more about *burakumin*, to learn the history and the present situation. I felt it was necessary for Ayako to understand in general the ways in which a dominant group attempts to control another group by defining them and degrading them. I wanted her to see the significance of stereotypes and other subtle forms of discrimination in the control they exert over the self-perception of one's group.

If Ayako could understand the nature of oppression, she could be free to define her own experience. She could engage in self-expression and empowerment through self-definition, which seeks to destroy the images created by the dominant group. She needed knowledge of the suffering, courage, and struggles of her own group and an understanding of her place in that group. I hoped that if she met others with the same background she could see her problem as more than just personal, as one that she shared with many others. I encouraged her to place herself in the context of a broader social situation.

Ayako's ambivalence was overcome when she decided that it was too important an opportunity to pass up and she persisted through the context of research projects to explore her background. She approached *burakumin* organizations and met political activists and scholars from whom she learned more about the reality of the conditions faced by *burakumin*. She was seeking identity resolution through social affirmation of her identity and association and support of members of the same group.

Ayako was stimulated by these encounters. "The people I met at the association were impressive. They have so much energy and enthusiasm. They are dedicated to eliminating prejudice. They asked me to join them and fight discrimination against *burakumin*. I think it's important, so I volunteered to help."

Now that she had named her struggle as a *burakumin* and accepted the label, she felt anger about oppression that *burakumin* have suffered and the irrationality of prejudice from majority Japanese. She was reflecting on herself as a cultural being and developing a keener sense of being *burakumin*.

However, Ayako's feelings again changed quickly through her actual experience of involvement. Her initial feelings of camaraderie were mixed with feelings of difference from those in the struggle. These insights gave us the chance to question the whole concept that there was a group called *burakumin* to which she belonged and was confined to.

"I can understand that the people I have met are dedicated, because they grew up being aware of the problems and had some bad experiences. But I feel really different. I mean, I told you that I have never been discriminated against. How can I understand what they are talking about? I sometimes wonder, am I really *burakumin*?"

I answered, "You don't have to be a victim to fight for victims. You just need the conviction that it is work that you should do. But, maybe it's not your struggle. Maybe you would be forcing yourself to be somebody you are not. If your life has not been filled with painful discrimination, maybe it is not your calling to devote your life to fighting it. I think you have come a long way in realizing that there is nothing at all shameful about your background. There is a lot to be proud of too in the courage of those who have fought discrimination. But there is a difference between realizing that there is no reason to feel ashamed of your background and making it the basis of your life."

Through my involvement in ethnic organizations, I realized that the idea of a minority group is as much of an imagined community as is a nation. A group is constructed out of widely diverse individuals for political purposes, and pressure is placed on individuals to regard this ethnic or racial group identity as somehow more authentic than other possible identities. But in Ayako's case would it really be an authentic identity?

STRUGGLING WITH QUESTIONS OF AUTHENTICITY

Throughout Ayako's searching, she struggled with deep identity questions. Identity development is not a smooth path onward and upward but a rocky road on which a person may swing wildly from one extreme position to another. Her moods fluctuated and her emotional stability wavered. Shortly before her 20th birthday, the ritual age of becoming an adult in Japan, Ayako made some suicidal gestures. She said she was tired of life, tired of being a good girl, tired of thinking. Cutting her wrists was shocking, and allowed her to forget her anguish for a moment; creating pain in the body eliminated pain in her mind. I became busy mobilizing friends to create a support network to help get her through her crisis.

During this period, I was struck by how Ayako would switch to speaking English when she was in the greatest torment. Since she fluctuated between using English and Japanese most of the time, I was surprised that she would revert to a second language when she was most disturbed. It seemed logical to assume the opposite—the reliance on one's native tongue when distressed. When I pointed this out to her, she said she had not noticed it, but somehow felt better speaking English at such moments. "I guess I'm struggling for some distance from my emotions, and English helps me to feel more in control over my feelings."

But control was difficult for her. Suddenly she wanted to tell everyone that she was *burakumin*. Perhaps motivated by a sense of guilt that she had not suffered enough to qualify as a genuine *burakumin*, she seemed to want to invite persecution. As much as I supported her in principle, I thought it was important to question the wisdom of her actions. During this period she needed constant reminders that this aspect of her heritage was only a part of her. And while the experiences of many individuals have been greatly influenced by this ancestry, for a person who had never suffered from discrimination perhaps it was a part that bore little personal significance.

I asked her, "Are you sure you want to tell everyone that you are *burakumin*? I mean is it really that much an important part of who you are? When you meet someone for the first time do you really have to introduce yourself as 'Hi, I'm Ayako the *burakumin*?'"

Ayako giggled self-consciously, "I just feel phony if I don't let them know."

"But just think how it sounds. 'Hi, I'm George, I'm gay!' 'Hi, I'm Irene, I'm a Christian.' 'Hi, I'm Bob, I'm half American, half Japanese, and half French.'"

I had her laughing now. Ayako liked my sense of humor.

I went on, "Maybe it's too private for a conversation starter. It's more than most people want to know. It might be just burdening them with something that they don't even care about. Maybe they are thinking, 'Why is this girl telling me this?' Have you thought about how you would like them to react? What would you want them to say?"

Ayako was unsure.

I struggled with my position here. Why was I encouraging her to conceal her background? As a psychologist with a social conscience, I believed in the importance of her coming out and challenging the consciousness of oppression. I believed that self-assertion is liberating to the spirit and a form of true living. If she had nothing to be ashamed of, why could she not tell anyone and everyone that she was *burakumin*? I wanted her to decide what was authentic for her, although I questioned whether there was one authentic self that she would discover, but rather thought she would find authenticity in different ways in different situations. I hoped that she could liberate herself from psychological chains of oppression and also live wisely. She had nothing to be ashamed of; society would change only by exploding these myths.

And on a more personal level I applauded her efforts to define herself. I too had gone through a period in which I wanted everyone I met to know I was Japanese and Irish. To my surprise, I found out that some people could care less, but I persisted in announcing it anyway. Should I encourage her in the same way? Many of my American friends whose status was ambiguous by their appearance resorted to various methods of self-revelation, some by names, others by hair style or clothing that announced their identity.

Yet I wanted to be careful not to impose my ideas on her. I had grown up in the United States, where my beliefs had fermented. Although many individuals hide their roots, it is also an openly multicultural society, where people of diverse backgrounds agree in principle to live together. In contrast to America's melting pot or salad bowl, pluralist ideology, Japan has insisted on a homogeneous national identity. I knew little of the pressures she would be under in Japanese society were she to reveal her background, nor did I know emotionally the feeling of some majority Japanese toward those they consider *burakumin*. In contrast to her situation, I am a highly visible minority, but one relegated these days mostly to the status of outsider rather than inferior.

IS IT BETTER TO LET IT BE?

In an attempt to deal with the issue on a broader level, I also decided to introduce the topic in a psychology class on prejudice. Although there are between 2 to 3 million *burakumin*, depending on who is counting, many young Japanese in parts of the country where there are no discriminated communities are unaware of their existence. It was in the second session on the topic that a student raised her hand and reminded me that the *burakumin* topic was one that Japanese consider better left unspoken. With uncharacteristic boldness and directness for my Japanese students, she told me with a mischievous grin that her mother had said that any teacher who talked about such things was an idiot. I smarted from her comment; I was being treated as a naïve and ignorant outsider making trouble. But I wondered if she might be right.

Was it better to let it be? Was I employing American methods of education in a society in which they didn't apply? Was it better to go along with the social expectation to treat the issue as unspeakable? Strong denunciation tactics by the Buraku Liberation League against discriminatory representations have intimidated publishers and television producers and inhibited the mentioning of the topic of *burakumin* in the press. Although it is generally permissible to use the word *burakumin* in English, the word itself is avoided and rarely used in either English or Japanese. But the avoidance of the subject has not eliminated prejudice and discrimination. Instead, the existence of these persons is covered with a dark veil of secrecy.

I hoped that this kind of education would explode myths and prejudices toward *burakumin*. But my student was warning me that education about the issue is filled with dangers. Another student explained that the education about *burakumin* that he had received in school had actually had the effect of making him prejudiced, by planting negative impressions in his mind. Because most *burakumin* pass in society as majority members, the students had no known experience to actually interact with *burakumin* and therefore felt a strange fascination and distance with them. Other students also complained that my well-intentioned efforts were counterproductive. They were happier and less biased, they insisted, when they were ignorant.

But other students supported my efforts to educate about *burakumin*. These students insisted that just covering up the issue will not make it go away. And I knew that the reality is that more than 100 years since emancipation people like Ayako may still be tormented by the knowledge of the status of their ancestors. In any case, I guided Ayako as she continued her research and presented it in her class without any problems arising.

TELLING HER BOYFRIEND

Later in the year Ayako came in with a troubled expression and gave me what should have been good news.

"I have a new boyfriend. He is kind and treats me well."

"So how come you don't look happy when you tell me about it?"

"Well, I have a problem. My mother thinks that I should tell him about my background. But I'm not so sure. She said it's better to find out now if it makes a difference to him. She says, "If you wait until you are really serious and tell him, you could be really hurt if he or his family rejects you.' I don't want to tell him because I don't think it's important who my ancestors were hundreds of years ago. But maybe she's right."

"I guess your mother is just hoping to protect you from some possible heartache by encouraging you to reveal your background earlier rather than later. Maybe the right moment will come and it will seem natural to tell him. Remember what you said—that if it makes a difference to him, he's not the kind of person you would want to be intimate with anyway."

Two weeks later the opportunity came and she told him.

"One night we were watching a program on Koreans in Japan on television and I felt that it was my chance. My heart was pounding so hard I was sure he could hear it, but I told him. He didn't react much but later he started to read some books about it and discuss them with me. I'm so relieved because there doesn't seem to be any problem. Of course, if we ever think about marriage I wonder if his attitude might change because of his family's reaction."

Ayako knew that although she was physically indistinguishable from majority Japanese, her boyfriend's family could easily discover her background even if she never mentioned it. Just as she had discovered it by simply checking her family register, his family could do the same through a private investigator. I have personally acquired family registers (of family members) in which I am not registered without having to prove my status as a relative.

And she knew from her studies that it might make a difference to them, even if he claimed no prejudice himself. Engagements and marriage plans are broken due to this discovery and resulting suicides are also not uncommon. These days family members usually claim that they personally are not prejudiced but are only concerned that the person's background could be damaging to the whole family, including the marriage plans of siblings. Thus fears of pollution linger and continue to lead to discrimination.

"I wonder how people really feel about it though," she said.

"Have you had any experiences that would lead you to believe that they harbor any feelings about *burakumin*?"

"Just recently I remembered something that happened a long time ago. Somehow I had forgotten it. But maybe all this study I am doing made me bring it up from my unconscious."

"When did it happen?"

"It was just after I found out about being *burakumin*."

"So you were around 14?"

"Yeah, I was still in junior high school. I was with my best friend, Yoko. I would play with her a lot at her house. Her parents ran a little store, so were always at home, whereas my mom was always at work. We were sitting in the living room and they were in the kitchen."

"What time of year was it?"

"It was winter, because I remember that we were sitting under the *kotatsu* [heating table] keeping warm."

"And eating mandarin oranges?"

Ayako laughed, because a classic image of traditional Japan is of people sitting under a *kotatsu* in winter eating mandarin oranges. "Yes, how did you know?"

"What else do people do sitting at *kotatsu*?" I joked. "Anyway, sorry to interrupt—so her parents were in the kitchen?"

"They were sitting at the kitchen table drinking tea and talking in kind of hushed voices. Yoko was talking too so I couldn't hear well. Once in a while one of them would glance toward us. Something about the way they talked made me want to listen. Yoko didn't seem to notice anything; she just went on gabbing about some boy that she liked."

"But you wanted to hear what her parents were saying?"

"Yes, I don't know why."

"Were you afraid they were talking about you?"

"I don't think so, because I heard the name Tanaka, who was a classmate of ours. Then I thought I heard the word *buraku* and thought that her parents looked over toward us. I strained to listen, but Yoko was talking excitedly. Then I saw her father flash a sign to her mother—four fingers. She nodded. They looked over at us again."

"Yotsu—the four-finger sign for *burakumin*?"

I had heard that that was a secret sign for *burakumin*—four fingers indicating the four legs of an animal.

"Was that sign what struck you the most?"

"Yes, it was a shock to see them do that."

"How did you feel?"

"Maybe like I felt when I first found out about my background. No . . . I don't know . . . maybe I was scared, thinking that they knew."

"How did you feel about Yoko and her parents?"

"I think I was afraid that they were not who I thought they were; like I couldn't trust them any more. Yoko wasn't prejudiced, she was my best friend and even if she knew, she would still be my best friend, but she might be influenced by her parents. What if they found out and told her and she hated me? I couldn't stand to think about it."

"It sounds like a strange and confusing situation to be put in," I told her. "Who your ancestors were in an ancient caste system hundreds of years ago should mean nothing today. And on the surface it doesn't but perhaps below the surface it does."

"I guess I was forced to see that it really is true; people do still care about being *burakumin*."

"When you reflect on that story now, what sense do you make of it? How do you feel about it now?"

"Well, I don't think they were talking about me. After that nothing ever happened. Yoko never acted weird and her parents still treated me the same. But I became a little more cautious, a little more aware that you never know what people might really feel about it. Normally, its just something that seems not to exist. But maybe its always there lurking beneath the surface of society."

MORE THAN JUST AN IDENTITY PROBLEM?

Throughout the year we continued to wrestle with the basic question of how she should deal with the reality of *buraku* status and discrimination on an individual level. What is the psychological cost of her secret? Should she aggressively assert her *burakumin* status to express her outrage at the indignity suffered by her ancestors and as a way of identifying with the oppressed? Or would it be wiser to recognize the damage that might occur in her life from casual revelations and therefore keep it a secret? Could she even reject its importance to her since she had never been affected by discrimination? Would she be able to overcome the old connotations of filth and degradation by discovering pride in the claims that exalted pillars of Japanese culture such as *kabuki* and *kyogen* were once the art of people of outcaste status?

But perhaps these questions were relatively not that deep for her, compared with someone who grew up in a life filled with prejudice and discrimination. After all, her formative years were not marked by traumatic encounters with racism. She had not been scarred when she was young and delicate by the brutal hands of hatred, and had grown up in the comforting belief that she was one of the majority. She had approached me with the problem of identity, but I was realizing that Ayako's problems were related to more than just her secret background.

The loss of her father as an infant and what she described as her mother's inability to respond emotionally to her as a child had affected Ayako deeply. We turned our attention to her attempts to create a new way of relating to her mother. Her suicidal gestures also seemed related to more than the

identity concerns of being *burakumin*. Their occurrence shortly before
the ritual of Coming-of-Age Day, the day of becoming an adult in Japan,
indicated Ayako's fear of becoming an adult. Her passage into adulthood
was particularly difficult, as she became acutely anxious about death. She
claimed that she wanted to remain a child and did not want to become
an adult and enter into that dirty world. She started to complain continually of physical ailments, either real or imagined. We needed to direct our attention to helping her cope with her feelings of the terror of
life, hypochondriasis, preoccupation with aging, the passage of time, and
death itself.

Ayako's image of childhood was that she had been a model child. She
was always good, pleasant, well-mannered, and praised widely for causing her mother no trouble.

"I was always a good girl, nice to everyone, good at everything, liked
by everyone. People always complimented me, 'You are such a good girl,'
'so responsible,' 'always taking care of yourself,' 'not causing your mama
any trouble!'"

"Were you really that good?" I asked in mock disbelief.

Ayako giggled. "Well, I wasn't perfect, but I guess I was a good girl."

"Well, that will make you tired!" I joked. "Why do you think you
needed to be such a good girl?"

"Maybe I didn't want to burden my mother; she had to work and raise
me alone. I could help her by being good, not causing trouble. People always mentioned that my mom was having a hard time too, so I should
help her out."

"That has been a heavy burden for you. To be good, to avoid to *amaeru*,
when you must have wanted to. But you're good at doing *amaeru* with
me."

Ayako laughed, "I can do it with some other people, but not with my
mother.

This was one of the occasions when a Japanese word just seemed to
fit better than any English equivalent. *Amae* is one of those words that seem
to portray a wide range of thoughts and behaviors that are heavily emphasized among Japanese people. We were describing her desire to indulge
in the kindness and benevolence of others.

When Ayako came to Tokyo for school, it was the first time she had
lived alone. She wanted to *amaeru*, but her calls to her mother were bit-
terly disappointing. Her mother seemed cold and distant.

"Maybe your mother is going through a hard time too," I suggested.

"What do you mean?"

"Maybe it's just as hard for her to be away from you."

"She doesn't act like it though."

"Well, she's a middle-aged Japanese woman, do you really expect her to show her feelings?" I chided. Ayako smiled, and I went on, "She's also alone for the first time. That might be just her way of adjusting to the demands of her new life and dealing with her feelings. She is trying to be strong, to let you go, to be alone. She wants you to be strong, not to rely on her so much."

Ayako was quiet for a moment, then said, "You know, there was a time when I really began to wonder if my mother loved me. Then when I went to the United States for a home stay the affectionate behavior of my American host mother surprised me and really impressed me. She would hug and kiss me and tell me I was wonderful. I couldn't help but compare her with my own mother who never hugged or kissed me . . . never praised me.

"Compared with my homestay mother, my mother was aloof, even cool, and seemed disinterested. When I was a child I tried hard to please her, but she never showed any enthusiasm for what I achieved. If I would get a good grade I would come home and show it to her, but she would just say, 'I guess you did your best.' I was always disappointed because she never seemed happy about my success."

"Well, Ayako, I used to notice the same thing when I was growing up in the States. You know that my mother is Japanese, and she wasn't like my friends' mothers; she wasn't cool like they were when they smoked Salems and wore tank tops. And she never showed any physical affection; she was more like your mom. I thought maybe she didn't love me as much as American mothers loved their kids. But I eventually came to realize that she just showed her feelings differently. She showed love by what she did for me, which was more than any other mother did for their kid, not by hugging me and praising me. Maybe your mother is showing her love in the only way she knows how."

Ayako's eyes showed me that she understood what I was saying.

"What would it be like to try to talk to your mother about these feelings?"

"Oh, we have never talked about this. She can't talk about feelings."

"Now that you can talk about your feelings, maybe you can give her another chance to try. If you show her how, maybe she can do it too."

One day Ayako came in and with a big smile told me that she had talked with her mother. She had expressed her feelings openly and asked her mother some hard questions.

"My mother told me that was always proud of me when I did something good, but she didn't want to praise me much because she wanted me to be strong and independent. She thought that if she praised me I would do things just to please her, rather than for myself. She didn't want me to study to get good grades to make her happy. But she wanted me to study because I enjoyed studying. She said that because I was an only child she thought I needed to be strong. Because there was no father she had to also act like a father."

Ayako was crying now. "I realized how hard it had been for her, raising a child all by herself. She had to be strong. It wasn't that she didn't love me."

Ayako understood herself and her mother much better now. She and her mother developed a new closeness and intimacy as two women, not only as mother and daughter. I saw her less and less as time went on and then she graduated and our only contact was through occasional phone calls and New Year's greeting cards.

KEEPING SECRETS

Years later when I saw Ayako she had clearly overcome her adolescent trauma. Perhaps the crisis would never have happened if she had gone to a Japanese university and remained in a Japanese environment. Her presence in the American university liberated her to confront her background and experiment with her identity. The atmosphere of openness and acceptance of diversity along with identification of prejudice and discrimination encouraged her to reveal her background and determine what that heritage meant.

Ayako achieved an acceptance of her background but lives with a fear that one day prejudice may appear to bedevil her. Through her searching for knowledge of her background, she has empowered herself with the understanding that she has no reason to feel shame or inferiority. Therapy was one safe place in which she revealed her secret to another individual and found that it had no negative impact on the relationship. Now she decides on a case-by-case basis to whom and when she will talk about her background, although she feels that it should not be kept from anyone with whom she becomes intimate. She no longer struggles constantly with these issues but lives quietly with her secret while most of those she meets consider her just another ordinary Japanese.

Among the few people she eventually revealed her secret to, she encountered no negative reactions. This acceptance may have convinced her that her background was, in fact, a nonissue to most people, at least to those she cared about the most and who care about her as well. In the years since, she has told no one but her present husband. She has still experienced no discrimination. As almost no one ever discusses the topic openly, she has not been exposed to any prejudicial attitudes.

But the issue remains in the shadows. Now she worries about her own children. "What should I tell them?" she asked.

"But you don't have any children," I chided.

Ayako laughed, "I know, but if I do, I'm just wondering what do I tell them about my, or their, background."

"Or by telling your children do you perpetuate something that has so little meaning?"

"That's what my husband says. He says, 'What's the point of telling them? They are no different than anyone else.'"

"But you know that if someone wanted to, they could find out about your kids' background."

"Yes, if they wanted to go to the trouble."

"Maybe it's as simple as telling them that some of their ancestors were discriminated against, like Jews would tell their children about the Holocaust, or African Americans tell their kids about slavery?"

Ayako gave me a look that said that we both knew it should be as simple as that, but somehow isn't. A *burakumin* past is shrouded in mystery. Its power lies in the taboo, the unspeakable.

Ayako has no other worries now. She is not and does not intend to be employed by a major company so the only other likely way of discrimination would be marriage. But she had told her boyfriend early in their relationship and it had made no difference to him. And now they were married.

"When my husband proposed to me, I was so happy I immediately called my mother to tell her. But just like with my previous boyfriend, she put a damper on my feelings right away by telling me that I had to force him to tell his parents right away. With a heavy feeling I hung up and called him and said, 'You have to tell your parents.' He was at their house at the time and promised he would do it right away. But I called him a few hours later and asked him, 'Did you tell them?' He admitted that he hadn't. I insisted he do it and hung up again. I waited, and some time later he called back. He had told his mother, he said. She said that she didn't care, but told him 'Don't tell your father.' So they decided to keep it a secret from him. I felt strange, but thought that I had to go along with whatever they decided as a family. He told me that his father would not attempt to investigate my family because his older brother and older sister's partners had not been investigated.

"My husband's father is really nice to me, so I feel bad not telling him. He is embarrassed by their financial condition now. We are much better off than they are. We own land and a house and my relatives have their own businesses. But his father clings to his samurai background as a symbol of his worth."

As I have done, too, I thought to myself, gradually realizing that the pride in one's elite background is a form of empowerment that is done at the expense of others to whom one feels superior. Relieving the monotony of equality and middle-class moderation in mundane daily existence with claims of past glory seems more pathetic to me now. And when this glory was not even one's own but simply one's ancestors, it rings empty with the hollowness of romantic longings and desires. Now I cringe when I hear people talk of their samurai ancestry, as those struggling for acceptance are apt to do. I tell no one of the ancestors I have never known.

Ayako was finishing her story. "When my mother met his parents it was really funny. His father said to my mother, 'Our family is poor now, but our blood line is without question pure and untainted.' My mother just smiled and nodded. Later when we got back to our hotel room we had a good laugh recalling what had happened.

"'So their blood is pure!' my mother joked. 'Well, if he only knew about ours!'"

CHAPTER 6

Epilogue

If I knew the way, I would take you home.

(Garcia & Hunter, 1970)

The stories in this book illustrate my attempts to help individuals of various cultural backgrounds deal with difficult problems of living. Counseling is presented as a powerful way of assisting human development through challenging and reworking old and established patterns of experiencing self, others, and the world. Counseling is also shown as an encounter that involves the self-understanding of the counselor as much as that of the client.

In the Prologue I emphasize the importance of challenging the mainstream American cultural standards on which academic psychology and counseling are based and that dictate what is regarded as normal and abnormal and what is considered therapeutically effective. Counselors are trained to strive to make clients more independent, told never to give advice, advised to avoid self-disclosure, and warned not to accept gifts. But these kinds of guidelines are based on cultural values that are not shared by everyone. In my work with people of different cultural backgrounds I have violated all of the above rules when it seemed to be appropriate for effective therapy.

I also stress at the beginning of this book my concern about how multicultural competence is commonly taught by a method that endows ethnic groups with cultural traits by ignoring differences and freezing culture. The resulting generalized knowledge may give the counselor confidence, but is of limited clinical usefulness when one is face-to-face with any real person. Worse, such knowledge can lead to distancing, objectifying, and the development of stereotypes that may impede good counseling.

The approach presented in this book is an alternative and complementary way of teaching about culture through narratives that describe the particulars rather than ascribe general cultural traits to any individual. By their very nature, they portray how the lives of persons of any cultural background are concerned with problems of existence—death, meaning, suffering, isolation—as well as the more mundane issues of daily life. Their lives may be deeply flavored by their cultures, but they are still human dramas and personal stories.

The narratives illustrate an integrative approach that requires balancing various theoretical perspectives of therapy. Although this approach might be called existential, constructivist, or multicultural, there is no certain technique or style advocated but rather a belief that what we do should be based on the uniqueness of the persons with whom we are engaged. The stories lack clear directives of how to do counseling, instead teaching through the demonstration of particular interactions with particular clients.

Repeated throughout the narratives is the view that multicultural counseling demands a consciousness more than a set body of knowledge or techniques. Training calls for the development of character rather than the acquisition of external labels of achievement. Counselors are challenged to see each person as a unique individual with human characteristics deeply flavored by particular cultural influences. Each counselor must develop his or her own way of working, creating a unique approach for each person with whom he or she is fortunate to engage.

I believe that it is important for each reader to derive his or her own meanings from these stories. However, many of us do not come from traditions in which storytelling is regarded as a valid form of teaching. Some readers may want more explicit explanation of what is being illustrated. And I realize that the concepts here may be difficult to grasp, as they lack the simplicity of approaches that claim that culture is either all or nothing. An integrative approach may seem like taking the best of all worlds, but synthesizing seemingly conflictual theoretical approaches may be confusing, and certainly lacks the clarity of following a particular style from one school.

Therefore, in this chapter I explain more specifically what occurred in these encounters by three themes. One is the attempt to understand the client's worldview. Another is the striving for a greater awareness of one's own worldview. And then there is the challenge of balancing these worldviews.

UNDERSTANDING THE CLIENT'S WORLDVIEW

The therapist should never assume he knows what the patient is talking about.
(Sullivan, quoted in Chapman, 1976, p. 208)

Counselors are continually trying to understand what clients are experiencing and feeling in the moment, as well as in what Kahn (1997) calls "the gradually unfolding coherence of the themes of their lives" (p. 168). The word *diagnosis* in its original and profound meaning of "thoroughly knowing" teaches us that the most important aspect of all healing is the effort to know our clients fully (Nouwen, 1966). Knowing is being able to observe and comprehend what is going on in the present in accurate, concrete, and complete detail.

However, just as our own pains are hard to touch, so are those of others, and just as we like to take the easy way ourselves, we also prefer to offer advice and treatment to others without having known the wounds that need healing. Still, it is not in the desire to change or to fix but in the willingness to know the other that we reach out and become healers. Therefore, counseling encompasses the creation of an empty and compassionate space where those who suffer can tell their story to someone who can listen with care (Welwood, 1983a). This is more than just a technique, and requires the full and real presence of the counselor.

Multicultural counseling presents the challenge of appreciating the worldview of those whom we consider culturally different—and the greater the differences, the greater the struggle (Pedersen, Fukuyama, & Heath, 1989). But apparent differences can make us more aware of the danger of assuming that we know and motivate us to ask our clients for their help when we don't understand. Although we may begin by naturally applying our own cultural standards as if they were universal, we can gradually refine and adapt them to identify culturally different worldviews (Segall, Dasen, Berry, & Poortinga, 1990).

Understanding the client's worldview helps us to construct stories that make sense of his or her behaviors and feelings and offer a resonant emotional response (Omer & Alon, 1997). This awareness also enhances the power of the stories that counselors tell to clients by enabling us to use metaphors based on shared experiences and understandings. Our attempts to use metaphors based only on general cultural knowledge are likely to be unconvincing or inappropriate. In my work with Hideo (Chapter 2), a city boy, nature metaphors fell flat, while those of shared racial experience resonated deeply.

Our attempts to understand a client's worldview are a form of respect. The Latin origin of the word, *respicere*, means to look at and see. Seeing someone as he or she is, and not as we would like him or her to be, is respecting that person (Fromm, 1956/1989). Without being seen where we are, humans find it hard to move and no matter how good the advice may be we defy the determined efforts of others to change us. Perry (quoted in Morimoto, 1993) describes how a battle for power and control ensues in which defenses go up and "options disappear, resistances arise, and creative efforts to prevent annihilation burst forth in a fight for one's existence" (p. 1).

When counselors think they know better than their clients what they should be doing in therapy, we consciously or unconsciously impose our cultural values on them. We move ahead too quickly in our desire to change the clients and abandon them in their struggles. But until they feel understood, clients cannot give up their battle and put their energy into moving on.

Our assumptions that clients are resisting, acting out, or defending against our best efforts to teach them may disappear when we consider the possibility that they know better than we do (Taft, 1973). If our efforts are directed instead toward allowing ourselves to feel what they are feeling, to enter their world as if it were our own, the possibility to learn about them and their cultures emerges. Sensing the client's tolerance for and capacity to integrate novel experiences of therapy is a skill complicated by cultural differences. Respect is expressed as patience, such as when we ask something we really need to know but are sensitive when the client does not wish to respond.

Counselors struggle to avoid reductionism, ridicule, denial of confusion, and other defenses of arrogance (Katz, 1999). But it is only to the degree that the counselor respects the person with whom he or she is working that the counselor can begin to understand the experienced reality of that person. Seeing the value and significance of an experience from within the world of the participants requires suspending our judgments and allowing the experiences to speak to us.

Counselors attempt to show their understanding through techniques like reflection, which are safe and give us the assurance that at least we are doing something. But techniques seem mechanical unless they have been integrated into the counselor's own self (Leitner, 1995). It is from the commitment to values such as truth, caring, respect, and humility that techniques derive their healing power.

Verbal techniques like reflection also do not work well in some cultural settings where it would be more appropriate to show understanding with silence, a nod of the head, a sigh, a smile, a joining of hands, fleeting eye contact, the shedding of a tear, or a warm touch on the shoulder rather than through verbal reflection or a penetrating gaze. With a client from any culture, empathy is felt most deeply and conveyed most convincingly when we put aside our own agenda and open ourselves to the client's experience. Our spontaneity may then emerge in a creative and personal way of communicating empathy at that moment (Welwood, 1983a).

Understanding the client's worldview means learning directly how his or her life is affected by a myriad of cultural experiences and sociopolitical influences of immigration, poverty, racism, stereotyping, and powerlessness (Sue et al., 1998). Awareness of how these factors impact the lives of our clients is a first step. However, textbook knowledge is unconvincing to clients who want to know if we have any life experience that enables us to at least begin to understand.

Ayako (Chapter 5) presented a formidable challenge of understanding the experience of an outcaste heritage that was to me only something I had read about. I had to draw on my own minority experience and general knowledge of minority psychology without presuming I understood her particular experience as a *burakumin*. I had to be especially careful with Hideo—a fellow mixed-blood—to not assume that I knew what he was experiencing.

Understanding the worldview of our clients includes reading the cues they give us and understanding the depth of emotions—processes that are complicated by different cultural norms (Neimeyer & Fukuyama, 1984). We may need to learn new cues, signals, and patterns of emotional expression because without knowing culturally learned criteria counselors cannot accurately interpret or evaluate behaviors and recognize emotions (Ivey, 1988).

Counseling is complicated with clients for whom the management and control of emotions is highly valued. Persons in many cultures have been socialized to believe that acceptance in a stoic and cheerful manner of the sad, even the tragic dimensions of life is admirable. Emotional distance is orchestrated in different cultures with dramatic variations in styles of experiencing and expressing emotions verbally and nonverbally.

Assuming that sadness is shown only by a dark countenance will lead us to mistake a smiling face for happiness. Yet people in some cultures commonly smile when talking about something painful or tragic. Ayako often giggled when uttering expressions of anguish. More than once I failed to recognize the extent of her emotional suffering, deluded by her smiles and verbal assurances that she was okay. Anger also has many faces, and we may not recognize it when it is hidden behind a calm demeanor. Khermani's (Chapter 3) anger was obvious, but when Hideo denied that he was upset when I cancelled an appointment, I didn't understand how angry he was until much later.

Understanding the client's worldview includes awareness of individual and cultural differences regarding authentic relationships. Counselors may lack an appreciation of silence and nonverbal forms of communication, having been trained in a method that is a verbal dialogue. Our professional training influences us to experience discomfort with some clients, wanting them to speak more and to move quickly through therapy. We value the articulation of the highly verbal client, yet nonverbal forms of communica-

tion as expressed in subtle gestures and powerful silences are greatly valued in some cultures where words are regarded as inadequate to express
the deepest human emotions (Kameguchi & Murphy-Shigematsu, 2001).

Introspection and self-disclosure are expected parts of therapy but the
ability of clients to engage in these activities varies greatly. Cultural norms
are dramatically different for the expression of an inner self in a spontaneous and open manner. The appropriate level of intimacy for counseling
will therefore also vary as well as the kind of intimate reflections and revelations we might expect (Roland, 1989). While there are those who can
quickly and easily express the private, inner, intimate world associated with
deep personal and family relations, others cannot. Those from more col-
lectivistic cultures are socialized to submerge the self in the interest of the
group and a personal focus is considered selfish or impolite. The expectations of the counselor that the client reflect deeply and reveal intimate
events and feelings may therefore be alien and inappropriate and cause
considerable anxiety for some clients (Vontress, Johnson, & Epp, 1999).
This requires regulating our level of openness and spontaneity and modifying our expectations for openness in clients according to their comfort
and readiness.

Establishing appropriate levels of intimacy in counseling is a complex,
culturally mediated process that requires understanding different worldviews. Counselors may try to adopt an informal stance that invites intimacy,
but this style may cause us to lose esteem with some clients. A formal style
in manner and dress may enhance our appearance of professionalism and
earn respect, especially with clients from more collectivist cultures who have
hierarchical expectations. However, this same style may create distance with
other clients. The challenge with each client is to establish a style that would
lead him or her to want to have a close relationship with you.

With bilingual clients it is important to understand how different lan-
guages are connected to worldviews. Speaking in Japanese to Hideo involved associations of formality, respect for hierarchical status, emotional
distance, and expectations of nonverbal understanding. English evoked
very different associations of autonomy, freedom, equalitarian relationships, and verbal expressiveness. The use of English in therapy therefore made it easier for us to communicate directly about issues dear to
him.

In our encounters with clients of various cultural backgrounds, differences inevitably emerge. Our efforts to overcome these differences can
be guided by a belief that cherishing each person's uniqueness, separateness, and wholeness transcends all other concerns (Morimoto, 1999). But
it is often our own fears that keep the person at a distance, forcing us to
reflect on our inner world.

AWARENESS OF OUR OWN WORLDVIEW

The psychotherapist, however, must understand not only the patient; it is equally important that he should understand himself.

(Jung, 1965, p. 134)

Through these stories I have tried to show how counselors bring their own worldviews to the relationship and how these affect the way they conduct therapy. Ideally counselors are actively engaged in the process of becoming aware of our own assumptions, values, biases, and preconceived notions about human behavior. We should be seeking a greater understanding of our cultural background, experiences, and worldview.

However, many of us have been trained to focus on the presumed defects of our clients rather than to look inside ourselves to see what we can offer (Breggin, 1997). Courage is required to confront personal issues when they arise in our work and to use them as opportunities for our personal growth. We need to find within ourselves the way to relate with interest, enthusiasm, and empathy to the person we are trying to help. Counselors also need to recognize the limits of our comfort with differences and how prejudice affects us in our work.

Acknowledging the feelings, beliefs, and stereotypes that we hold toward others is not easy, but must be done in order to recognize the impact we have on clients. Certain types of people antagonize us and certain styles of communication make us uncomfortable. We are challenged to actively foster self-awareness of negative emotional reactions and projections around race, gender, and culture that are detrimental to counseling and are reflected in our work with culturally different clients.

Cultivating greater self-awareness enhances our development as therapists since our ability to understand the experience of our clients is limited by the depth and range of our personal experience and insight. Counselors are given the opportunity to learn valuable lessons not only about others, but also about ourselves. In this kind of relationship of co-construction of reality two people work together to find new meaning and new ways of being (Ivey, 1986). Counselors become students and clients become teachers. This kind of therapy involves the counselor's working through and developing understanding about problems that arise from his or her own self-narratives.

Some of the multicultural literature gives the impression that our only task is to educate White people to be more aware of their racism (Wilson, 1994a). However, prejudices and biases are a part of any counselor's cultural baggage and it is important to examine them (Sue, 1993). The multicultural training that I received failed to force minority psychologists to address our own prejudices that arise in our work with Whites and with other minorities. But any of the multiple selves of a counselor of any ethnic background involving gender, class, race, or education may be salient at any particular moment and impact on the relationship with the client.

Counselors struggle to extend our capacity for understanding and accepting what is different by integrating foreign ways of thinking and experiencing. In this way we stretch the limits of self by embracing the otherness of the exotic, strange, and alien. As I attempted to discover how to help Ayako become liberated, I was forced to tangle with my own self-constructions. I became aware that while regarding myself as an oppressed minority, I had ironically empowered myself through my connections with a glorious past of class privilege. This narrative clashed dramatically with her attempt to liberate herself from the chains of this same feudal caste system. The same reality that empowered me oppressed her. This awareness forced me into a confrontation with one of the fragile narratives on which I had built my identity.

Self-awareness is also important because good intentions of the counselor do not necessarily lead to good consequences (Ridley, Mendoza, Kanitz, Angermeier, & Zenk, 1994). I chose a clinical residency in an inner-city hospital in a Black community because I romanticized African American culture and poverty. At first I refused to see abuse or pathology even when it was obvious, while a fellow trainee, who was working there reluctantly, on the other hand, saw pathology everywhere. But I became troubled when persons I was interviewing told me about terrible experiences of violence and abusive relationships they were in with spouses, lovers, or children, who happened to be Black, not White. To acknowledge such abuse threatened the claims to moral superiority associated with the suffering of and discrimination against Blacks. I feared that I might be mistakenly basing my intuition on a stereotype of chaotic families and abuse in African Americans, and that it is not right to further stigmatize an already oppressed minority group. The result was that my clinical intuition was compromised not only by potential cultural misunderstanding but also by a kind of self-censorship.

I tell this story to emphasize that our worldview is damaging to clients in unanticipated ways. My ability to help Hiromi (Chapter 4) was limited by my middle-aged cynicism of youthful identity conflicts. Empathizing with Hideo was made difficult by my own narrative of stoicism in the face of discrimination.

Self-knowledge brings to awareness our own stories, which may enhance our understanding of the client and also enable us to tell powerful stories to them. To tell a story we must experience it to the best of our ability and give up our worldviews and allow others to express theirs. Vulnerability involves a radical questioning of one's worldview—assumptions about what is "valid," "correct," "obvious," and "common practice" (Katz, 1999).

Experiencing moments of being between worldviews or realizing the multiplicity of valid worldviews is deeply disturbing and can shake the foundations of our being. Although it is painful, when we understand and accept our vulnerability it opens the door to self-knowledge and creates the possibility of understanding the world from within another culture. A therapist's connection with a client depends on somehow being vulnerable with that person (Welwood, 1983b). Embracing vulnerability can allow us to live inside another culture and become better able to tell its stories.

Acceptance of others is ultimately about self-understanding (Kristeva, 1993). We learn to accept others by realizing our own disturbing otherness, which threatens our attempts to maintain a proper, solid "I." Otherness is not simply something that exists on the outside, but also exists within.

BALANCING WORLDVIEWS

Balance in cognitive theory means changing, ignoring, differentiating, resolving, or transcending inconsistencies to avoid dissonance. In non-Western cultures, balance is often described as "asymmetrical," defined by tolerating inconsistency and dissonance rather than resolving differences to achieve apparent consistency.

(Pedersen, 1997, p. 287)

The ability to tolerate ambiguity, inconsistency, and dissonance may be one of the most difficult but necessary skills of counseling persons of different cultural backgrounds. Balance is a construct in multicultural counseling that involves the identification of diverse or even conflicting culturally learned perspectives without necessarily resolving the differences (Pedersen, 1990). Recognizing that we all depend on a culturally embedded, interpersonally connected, and necessarily limited perspective of reality, we are challenged to suspend assumptions that one view must be right and one wrong, and allow each to make valuable contributions to our understanding (Pedersen & Ivey, 1993). Various struggles emerge in our attempts at simultaneously understanding both the client's worldview and our own, and balancing these issues is an art of therapy.

Acceptance and Change

One major theme presented in the stories regards the conflict between acceptance and change. Counseling emphasizes change and liberation from oppression and the attempt to empower clients to engage in proactive behavior that challenges not only their own personal limitations, but also those of society. There is a strong tendency to value change itself as intrinsically good, and moving toward a solution and reconciling ambiguity are often goals of counseling.

But some other societies have cultural traditions that are based on philosophies of acceptance. Zen Buddhism is one such philosophy and indigenous therapies in Japan such as *Morita* and *Naikan* reflect this value of accepting things as they are, not the way we want them to be. Acceptance, as surrendering to that which is beyond our control, is regarded as paradoxically liberating the spirit to move on (Roland, 1989). Resignation as well as triumph has a place in concepts of healing, and change is not inevitably a positive and good outcome of therapy (Pedersen, 1997).

Neither change nor acceptance is without danger of excess. Change for its own sake can be empty or damaging. Acceptance of oppressive conditions can be passive resignation. A balanced perspective requires that we recognize that there are limitations on how much a culture accepts personal change and development. This means balancing a value of individual satisfaction and free choice with a respect for the individual as embedded in family and society. A belief in the necessity of personal responsibility for present actions and therapeutic change must be balanced with an awareness of the blame that can be attributed to others and society itself for one's problems.

My work with Hiromi most vividly brought this struggle alive for me. I believed strongly in the need to openly fight against ethnic bigotry and oppression and therefore hoped that she would openly flaunt her Korean ancestry and throw it in the face of those who would have preferred her silent acquiescence to the social rule of hiding one's minority background. Her ultimate decision that a name change was not authentic and self-defeating because other people, including her own family, were not ready for it was based on an understanding of herself and her society that I had to respect.

We often desire to change and repair our clients as if they were an object to be fixed, if we could only find the right parts. But trust is developed when we let the other be, and clients learn they can be with another person and be respected for who they are, as is. Such are the times that give them hope that they can find new possibilities in life (Shainberg, 1983).

Knowledge and Intuition

Knowledge of psychological theory as well as the various life experiences, cultural heritage, and historical background of the reference groups of the person we are trying to understand can serve as a general guide for our encounter. We should have some understanding of how race, culture, or ethnicity may affect personality formation, vocational choices, psychological disorders, help-seeking behavior, and the appropriateness of counseling approaches. Our ignorance of cultural differences will bring denial, intolerance, and bigotry into the counseling room (Ponterotto & Pedersen, 1994).

However, the knowledge that we acquire must not become oppressive and inhibiting of the intuitions that come to us in the actual face-to-face encounter. Supposedly factual information on cultural differences that exist between groups may make it seem impossible to bridge the gaps. Therefore, I am suggesting that we strive for a state in which we balance this knowledge with our intuitions to flexibly allow ourselves to engage with, and learn from, the individual before us in as unbiased a manner as possible.

If we want to know the meaning of their stories for our clients, it is fruitful to try to listen carefully for what we don't know. When we instead ask questions from a position of already understanding, the client's story is replaced by our professional account (Gergen & Kaye, 1996). Our diagnostic theoretical filters can easily control the information we are receiving, matching theory to client, past to present, and allowing in only what validates our ideas. What we observe follows from our theory and we can expand the space of our search until our answer is discovered (Spence, 1984). Our efforts to maintain curiosity, openness to the novel discovery, or flexibility to entertain the previously unconsidered depend on trying to put ourselves in the place of our clients.

It is tempting to naively trust in our own perceptions as unbiased, and rest assured that we know what is wrong with, and what is best for, our client. It is alluring to fall back on Freud, Jung, Rogers, Beck, or other gurus for determined answers, and take refuge in what we think we know, covering our discomfort by applying theory and interpretation (Yalom, 1989). Sullivan challenges counselors to be as flexible as possible in engaging with clients, even though the direction is unpredictable because human difficulties are too variable to allow dogmatic generalizations (in Chapman, 1976).

Our knowledge of general cultural characteristics, like any theoretical knowledge, can begin to fill in the gaps in the stories we are being told with unwarranted assumptions rather than encouraging us to know more to be able to understand. A position of "not knowing" (Anderson & Goolishian, 1996) does not mean that the study of psychological theories or ethnic groups is meaningless and should be abandoned. It is rather a warning that the knowledge we hold is of the process of therapy or of social and political conditions, but not of the content of individual people's lives (Freedman & Combs, 1996).

My attempt to balance knowing and not-knowing with Hideo meant struggling to let my knowledge of ethnic identity development inform, but not control, my contact with him. I tried not to fit Khermani into a psychiatric classification and to remain open to learning from him about his experience.

Levity and Gravity

Clients are often weighed down by feelings of the heaviness and seriousness of life. Counselors may try to convince clients to discover purpose and meaning in their lives, and recognize that they have a unique job that no one else can do. On the other hand, we may encourage them to see themselves as wider and deeper than the problems they carry around. We may help them to deal with events to which they have given a life-and-death quality by reducing its importance in the universe and trying to convince them not to take things so seriously. We may want to get them to lighten up, to see the humor in life, to laugh at themselves.

Balancing optimism and pessimism is therefore a source of tension. Without hope, therapy is powerless. The connections of hope and health are increasingly being documented and optimism is recognized as a form of emotional intelligence that enhances well-being and human relations (Goleman, 1997). But too much optimism may deprive some persons of the necessity of seeing themselves and their situation clearly. Practical solutions become difficult when the client indulges in excessive and false hope. Therefore, in the stories that clients construct we hope for a balancing of the negative and the positive. The persons in these stories could acknowledge what they had gained only if they also directly faced the losses that they had suffered. Such therapeutic splitting encourages clients to see both sides as inseparable and complementary (Omer & Alon, 1997).

Optimism and pessimism must also be balanced when counselors assess the importance of our role. Considering the myriad factors that weigh on an individual's life, we can never be sure of the impact we have had on a client. Remaining humble while experiencing ourselves as effective is also a matter of changing the perspective from "either-or" to "both-and"—we are both helpful and limited in our power to heal (Lipchik, 1993). A lack of faith in our ability is obviously self-defeating. But an unjustified sense of our own importance in healing our clients will cause us to miss opportunities to empower them.

With the clients in these stories I try to offer the hope that they might move in the way they wish, while also admonishing them that much would remain the same. This message is not given in a negative manner, but as a balanced and respectful assessment. When I told Hideo that he would become more able to engage with others, but probably never be the life of the party, he was finally able to laugh at himself. Khermani was sobered as I encouraged him to face both the damage to his career that could not be undone and the joy of awakening to his emotional life.

The Taoist philosophy of Yin and Yang as contrasting but complementary forces of female and male principles is expressed in the concept of asymmetrical balance that recognizes the necessary presence of both light and dark to provide meaning (Pedersen, 1997). This view of balance describes a harmonious tension between these principles, and humans as part of a dynamic order and relational design where all elements serve a necessary function. Applied to our daily lives, a sense of balance means touching the deepest existential questions as well as dealing with the mundane tasks and developing the full capacity for joy and sadness.

Similarities and Differences

These narratives demonstrate my attempts at maintaining a view that humans are simultaneously similar and different. This may seem simplistic, but I believe that our sensitivity to clients depends on balancing these perspectives. An understanding of shared humanity is essential to counseling. At the same time, we must have awareness that a person has something in common with certain other humans, which we call a shared culture. While balancing these perspectives, we must also attempt to recognize the uniqueness of the person before us. The clients in this book demonstrate how individual, group, and universal levels of identity are fluid. A client may focus on individual needs at one moment, at another on an issue related to reference group identity, while at still another time on universal human experience. The counselor flexibly strives to relate to that which is most salient at that moment.

Traditionally, counseling is engaged at primarily the individual or universal levels, thereby negating the important influences of reference groups. In reaction to this neglect, many of those promoting the field of multicultural counseling have strongly emphasized the importance of what is cultural and racial. In so doing, they have usually ignored what is idiosyncratic, although some have argued for the recognition of both perspectives (Locke, 1990). Sue (1990) has contributed heavily to a culture-specific approach, but he also warns of the dangers of this method leading to overemphasis on technique, objectifying clients, and developing racial and cultural stereotypes. While advocating the crucial importance of culture, Vontress (1979, 1996) has also continually stressed the significance of recognizing that people are more alike than different and that clients often consult us about problems in living that transcend culture and have little or nothing to do with race or ethnicity.

The debate over whether people are similar or different is logical dichotomy removed from reality (Lebra, 1992). Difference and sameness are not mutually exclusive and both clearly exist and must be understood to know a client's cultural contexts. There are obviously similarities of shared values across cultural groups and differences in how each expresses those values. But counseling, research, and writing are political acts that require us to take a stand. Which stand we take depends on our purpose and our audience. As these change, so does our focus. When I envision my purpose as fighting against the cultural biases in psychology and my audience as Whites who need to be convinced of the importance of race and culture, I must emphasize differences. If I turn my attention to those who are aware of these issues, my focus may shift to similarities.

Too much focus on either/or dichotomies of any kind can mislead counselors. The popular individualistic and collectivist duality disguises the existence of these values in each individual to various degrees. Persons from collectivist cultures may have learned to submerge a self to conform to group norms, but there is likely to be another self that longs for expressions of individuality.

I have personally found it helpful to emphasize the belief that we are more alike than we are different, or more human than anything else. A basic recognition that humans share concerns about living and dying must underlie the relationship that we hope to establish with any person who comes to us for help. Empathy depends on feeling this common ground and common bond that connects us to all other people regardless of the apparent differences. I would therefore prefer to err on the side of emphasizing our human commonalties, rather than induce the alienating and divisive feeling of overemphasizing our differences.

However, this focus may work for me as a balancing effect, since so much of my awareness is naturally placed on culture and race. I am a person who grew up in an extended family in which there were clear cultural differences between the Irish, the Japanese, and those mixed. I have lived much of my life in communities in which my family and I were strikingly different from others. But for someone without either experience or awareness of the powerful impact of racial and cultural differences in an individual's

life, it may be necessary to maintain a focus on differences in his or her work
to avoid denial and neglect of these crucial factors.

Linear and Fluid

Mainstream theories of development define a steady progression in
clear stages through which persons pass, each higher than the one before.
In Piagetian models of development, processes are unidirectional and hierarchical. Models of ethnic identity development delineate clear stages
through which persons pass, each more advanced in terms of cognitions
and behaviors than the previous. These models can serve as a guide for
understanding the concerns of our clients, providing insight into the prob-
able conflicts and possible sources of resolution of developmental crises.

However, development is not simply a linear path, nor are these models
necessarily valid for all individuals of all cultural backgrounds (Murphy-
Shigematsu, 1999, 2001a). Identity is increasingly seen as a fluid, unpredictable, cyclical, and uncategorizable process (Parham, 1989). Our understanding of the narrative nature of a life demands more flexible ways
of comprehending identity and recognition that experience does not follow a universal and irreversible order. Counselors are challenged to criti-
cize this hierarchical framework while integrating cultural identity theory
more directly into helping practice that is liberating and contributes to
consciousness development (Ivey, 1995).

A transformational model of development is described by Katz (1999)
as movement through transitions in which one alternates between increasing clarity and ambiguity of comprehension in a recurring process. The
boundaries between transitions are flexible without articulated end points
toward which they progress and culminate. One cycles through experiences
of insight and those in which we alter our daily context as a result of those
insights. We move both toward and away from meaning, balance, connect-
edness, and wholeness and there is a continued tension and struggle around
these issues. Each transition is a valued part of human development.

Development may also be understood through narratives of individuals' lives (Steenbarger, 1991). The stories that we tell can detail the ways
in which the self responds to accommodate changes in the sociocultural
context and assists the person to construct and reconstruct meaningful
reality. Narrative analysis of development, including ethnic identity development, may provide meaningful insights unobtainable through the
stage theory approach (Yi & Shorter-Gooden, 1999).

Counselors are challenged to actively embrace the tension that
exists between conflicting ideas. In the same way that we ask our clients

to integrate seemingly separate and supposedly opposing ideas, we must be able to do the same. Therapy itself might be described as a dynamic balance of movement that is simultaneously goal-oriented and without directionality. Although therapist and clients usually see it as having a clear direction of desired movement defined by an explicit destination, we know that this is not actually true (Yalom, 1989). Our movement in therapy is often unpredictable, without a clear course and constantly changing along with evolving circumstances. We often stumble blindly in the dark hoping for a glimmer of light. In therapy the work is on-going, there is no one way, one never knows for sure, and it is in the experience of mutual participation of discovery that healing takes place (Shainberg, 1983).

TRAVELERS AND GUIDES

The big question is whether you are going to be able to say a hearty yes to your adventure . . . the adventure of the hero—the adventure of being alive.
(Campbell, 1988, p. 163)

Life is often imagined as a journey, and we humans as the heroes of our own personal journeys (Campbell, 1960). Our lives are poetically por-trayed as movement along paths, down roads, or up streams. Romantic images of our travels, take us through woods, over mountains, and across oceans (Mahoney, 1995). While we are all travelers, some of us attempt to assist others in their journeys by becoming therapists or counselors.

In these stories I have shown my attempts as a counselor at guiding others in their journeys. Regardless of their cultural backgrounds, I started by respecting and attempting to see and know them as fully as possible. I listened to their stories of where they had come from and where they now were. I tried to help them discover where they wished to go, liberate them-selves from old chains, and walk down the road with a new narrative of their lives and new meaning—more whole, connected, and balanced.

It was never a simple matter of taking them where they wanted to go, because I myself did not know the way. I could accompany them for a while and trust in their ability to find their way and walk their path alone. I believed that each had a path that he or she must persistently attempt to rediscover and follow, though it twists and turns and clients are repeat-edly swayed and lured from it (Katz, 1999).

I tried to help with the understandings and intuitions that came when I was able to enter into and share their thoughts and feelings. Sometimes I had traveled a similar path and I revealed whatever insights or wisdom I had gained when the person seemed ready to hear it.

And because I am a fellow traveler, their troubles resonated deeply within me. In attempting to offer something, I needed to reach inside to a space where I face the same dilemmas and alternatives. Their struggles became my struggles.

We drifted and strayed and were bewildered at times, but I trusted that though we wandered we were not lost. I was guided by their voices, attempted to comfort when they were frightened and to encourage when they were despairing. I heartened them to consider that we are more than our problems, our bodies, and our egos.

I let them know that though I would be responsible, the ultimate responsibility is theirs. I urged them to live in the moment rather than in dreams of reaching some destination. Then one day we let go of each other's hands and said goodbye. And I accepted their gratitude and thanked them too when we parted at the fork in the road.

References

Abu-Lughod, L. (1991). Writing against culture. In R. G. Fox (Ed.), *Recapturing anthropology: Working in the present* (pp. 137–162). Santa Fe, NM: School of American Research Press.

Allport, G. W. (1962). The general and the unique in psychological science. *Journal of Personality, 30,* 405–422.

Anderson, H., & Goolishian, H. (1996). The client is the expert: A not-knowing approach to therapy. In S. McNamee & K. J. Gergen (Eds.), *Therapy as social construction* (pp. 25–39). London: Sage.

Appadurai, A. (1988). Putting hierarchy in its place. *Cultural Anthropology, 3,* 36–49.

Breggin, P. R. (1997). *The heart of being helpful: Empathy and the creation of a healing presence.* New York: Springer.

Bruner, J. (1990). *Acts of meaning.* Cambridge, MA: Harvard University Press.

Campbell, J. (1960). *The hero with a thousand faces.* New York: Meridian.

Campbell, J. (with B. Moyers). (1988). *The power of myth.* New York: Anchor.

Chapman, A. H. (1976). *Harry Stack Sullivan: The man and his work.* New York: Putnam.

Chow, R. (1993). *Writing diaspora: Tactics of intervention in contemporary cultural studies.* Bloomington: Indiana University Press.

Clifford, J. (1980). Review of orientalism, by Edward Said. *History and theory, 19,* 204–223.

De Vos, G. (1982). Afterword. In D. K. Reynolds, *Quiet therapies: Japanese pathways to personal growth* (pp. 113–132). Honolulu: University of Hawaii.

Dyson, M. E. (1995). Essentialism and the complexities of racial identity. In D. T. Goldberg (Ed.), *Multiculturalism: A critical reader* (pp. 218–229). Oxford: Blackwell.

Efran, J. S., & Clarfield, L. E. (1996). Constructionist therapy: Sense and nonsense. In S. McNamee & K. J. Gergen (Eds.), *Therapy as social construction* (pp. 220–210). London: Sage.

Freedman, J., & Combs, G. (1996). *Narrative therapy: The social construction of preferred realities.* New York: W. W. Norton.

Freire, P. (2000). Cultural action for freedom. *Harvard Educational Review, Monograph Series, 1.*

Fromm, E. (1989). *The art of loving.* New York: Harper Collins. (Original work published 1956)

Garcia, J., & Hunter, R. (1970). Ripple [Recorded by the Grateful Dead]. On *American Beauty* [LP]. Burbank, CA: Warner.

Gergen, K. J., & Kaye, J. (1996). Beyond narrative in the negotiation of mean-
    ing. In S. McNamee & K. J. Gergen (Eds.), *Therapy as social construction* (pp. 65–
    89). London: Sage.
Gilroy, P. (1995). Roots and routes: Black identity as an outernational project. In
    H. W Harris, H. C. Blue, & E. E. H. Griffith (Eds.), *Racial and ethnic identity:
    Psychological development and creative expression* (pp. 15–30). London: Routledge.
Goleman, D. (1997). *Emotional intelligence.* New York: Bantam.
Goncalves, O. F. (1995). Hermeneutics, constructivism, and cognitive-behavioral
    therapies: From the object to the project. In R. A. Neimeyer & M. J. Mahoney
    (Eds.), *Constructivism in psychotherapy* (pp. 195–230). Washington, DC: Ameri-
    can Psychological Association.
Good, B. J. (1998, May 7). *Culture and psychotherapy: Clinical issues in cross-cultural
    settings.* Paper presented to the Transcultural Psychiatry Association of Japan,
    Wakayama, Japan.
Harter, S. L. (1995). Construing on the edge: Clinical mythology in working with
    borderline processes. In R. A. Neimeyer & M. J. Mahoney (Eds.), *Constructivism
    in psychotherapy* (pp. 371–383). Washington, DC: American Psychological
    Association.
Hayes, R. L. (1994). Counseling in the postmodern world: Origins and implica-
    tions of a constructivist developmental approach. *Counseling and Human De-
    velopment, 72*(6), 1–12.
Hayes, R. L., & Oppenheim, R. (1997). Constructivism: Reality is what you make
    it. In T. Sexton & B. Griffin (Eds.), *Constructivist thinking in counseling practice,
    research, and training* (pp. 19–40). New York: Columbia University Press.
Held, B. S. (1995). *Back to reality: A critique of postmodern theory in psychotherapy.*
    New York: W. W. Norton.
Howard, G. S. (1991). Culture tales: a narrative approach to thinking, cross-
    cultural psychology, and psychotherapy. *American Psychologist, 46,* 187–197.
Ivey, A. E. (1986). *Developmental therapy: Theory into practice.* San Francisco: Jossey-
    Bass.
Ivey, A. E. (1988). *Intentional interviewing and counseling: Facilitating client develop-
    ment.* Pacific Grove, CA: Brooks/Cole.
Ivey, A. E. (1995). Psychotherapy as liberation. In J. G. Ponterotto, J. M. Casas,
    L. A. Suzuki, & C. M. Alexander (Eds.), *Handbook of multicultural counseling*
    (pp. 53–72). Thousand Oaks, CA: Sage.
Ivey, A. E., Ivey, M. B. & Simek-Morgan, L. (1997). *Counseling and psychotherapy:
    A multicultural perspective.* Boston: Allyn & Bacon.
Jung, C. J. (1965). *Dreams, memories, and reflections.* New York: Vintage.
Kabat-Zinn, J. (1995). *Wherever you go, there you are: Mindfulness meditation in every-
    day life.* New York: Hyperion.
Kahn, M. (1997). *Between therapist and client: The new relationship.* New York:
    W. H. Freeman.
Kameguchi, K., & Murphy-Shigematsu, S. (2001). Family psychology and family
    therapy in Japan. *American Psychologist, 56,* 65–70.
Kaptchuk, T. J. (1983). *The web that has no weaver.* New York: Congdon and Weed.

Katz, R. (1999). *The straight path of the spirit: Ancestral wisdom and healing traditions in Fiji*. Rochester, VT: Inner Traditions.

Kristeva, J. (1993). *Nations without nationalism* (L. S. Raudiez, Trans.). New York: Columbia University Press.

La Fromboise, T., & Foster, S. L. (1989). Ethics in multicultural counseling. In P. Pedersen, J. Draguns, W. Lonner, & J. Trimble (Eds.), *Counseling across cultures* (3rd ed., pp. 115–136). Honolulu: University of Hawaii Press.

Lebra, T. S. (1992). Self in Japanese culture. In N. Rosenberger (Ed.), *Japanese sense of self* (pp. 105–120). Cambridge: Cambridge University Press.

Leitner, L. M. (1995). Optimal therapeutic distance: A therapist's experience of personal construct psychotherapy. In R. A. Neimeyer & M. J. Mahoney (Eds.), *Constructivism in psychotherapy* (pp. 357–370). Washington, DC: American Psychological Association.

Lipchik, E. (1993). "Both/and" solutions. In S. Friedman (Ed.), *The new language of change: Constructive collaboration in psychotherapy* (pp. 25–49). New York: Guilford.

Locke, D. (1990). A not so provincial view of multicultural counseling. *Counselor Education and Supervision, 30*, 18–25.

Mahoney, M. J. (1995). The psychological demands of being a constructivist psychotherapist. In R. A. Neimeyer & M. J. Mahoney (Eds.), *Constructivism in psychotherapy* (pp. 385–399). Washington, DC: American Psychological Association.

May, R. (1969). *Love and will*. New York: W. W. Norton.

Mio, J. S., & Awakuni, G. I. (1999). *Resistance to multiculturalism: Issues and interventions*. London: Brunner/Mazel.

Morimoto, K. (with J. Gregory and P. Butler). (1972). *On trying to understand the frustrations of students*. Cambridge, MA: Bureau of Study Counsel, Harvard University.

Morimoto, K. (1993). *Stay on the court*. Unpublished manuscript.

Morimoto, K. (1999). *My present philosophy of life*. Unpublished manuscript.

Morita, S. (1998). *Morita therapy and the true nature of anxiety-based disorders (Shinkeishitsu)*. Albany: State University of New York Press.

Murphy, F. P. (1991). *Going through the wood: The poems of Fred Murphy*. Tokyo: Toshi Press.

Murphy-Shigematsu, S. (1999). Counseling minorities in Japan: Social and cultural context. *American Journal of Orthopsychiatry, 69*(4), 482–494.

Murphy-Shigematsu, S. (2001a). Cultural psychiatry and minority identities in Japan: A constructivist narrative approach to therapy. *Psychiatry, 63*(4), 364–385.

Murphy-Shigematsu, S. (2001b). *An ethnography of a Toyoigaku medical clinic in Japan*. Unpublished manuscript.

Neimeyer, G. J., & Fukuyama, M. (1984). Exploring the content and structure of cross-cultural attitudes. *Counselor Education and Supervision, 23*(3), 214–224.

Neimeyer, R. (1993). An appraisal of counstructivist therapy. *Journal of Consulting & Clinical Psychology, 61*(2), 221–234.

Neimeyer, R. (1995). Constructivist psychotherapies: Features, foundations, and future directions. In R. A. Neimeyer & M. J. Mahoney (Eds.), *Constructivism in psychotherapy* (pp. 11–38). Washington, DC: American Psychological Association.

Nouwen, H. J. M. (1966). *Reaching out: The three movements of the spiritual life*. Garden City, NY: Doubleday and Company.

Omer, H. (1998). Using therapeutic splits to construct empathic narratives. In M. F. Hoyt (Ed.), *The handbook of constructive therapies: Innovative approaches from leading practitioners* (pp. 428–448). San Francisco: Jossey-Bass.

Omer, H., & Alon, N. (1997). *Constructing therapeutic narratives*. Northvale, NJ: Jason Aronson.

Parham, T. (1989). Cycles of psychological nigrescence. *The Counseling Psychologist, 17*(2), 187–226.

Parry, A., & Doan, R. E. (1994). *Story re-visions: Narrative therapy in the postmodern world*. New York: Guilford.

Pedersen, P. (1990). Complexity and balance as criteria of effective multicultural counseling. *Journal of Counseling and Development, 5*, 550–554.

Pedersen, P. (1997). *Culture-centered counseling interventions: Striving for accuracy*. Thousand Oaks, CA: Sage.

Pedersen, P., Fukuyama, M. A., & Heath, A. (1989). Client, counselor, and contextual variables in multicultural counseling. In P. Pedersen, J. Draguns, W. Lonner, & J. Trimble (Eds.), *Counseling across cultures* (3rd ed., pp. 23–53). Honolulu: University of Hawaii Press.

Pedersen, P., & Ivey, A. E. (1993). Culture-centered counseling and interviewing skills. Westport, CT: Greenwood/Praeger.

Pierce, C. M. (1970). Offensive mechanisms. In F. Barbour (Ed.), *The black seventies* (pp. 71–83). Boston: Porter Sargent.

Ponterrotto, J. G., & Casas, J. M. (Eds.). (1991). *Handbook of racial/ethnic minority research*. Springfield, IL: Charles C. Thomas.

Ponterotto, J. G., & Pedersen, P. B. (1994). *Preventing prejudice: A guide for counselors and educators* (Multi-cultural aspects of counseling, Vol. 2). Thousand Oaks, CA: Sage.

Reynolds, D. K. (1982). *Quiet therapies: Japanese pathways to personal growth*. Honolulu: University of Hawaii Press.

Ridley, C. R., Mendoza, D. W., Kanitz, B. E., Angermeier, L., & Zenk, R. (1994). Cultural sensitivity in multicultural counseling: A perceptual schema model. *Journal of Counseling Psychology, 41*(2), 125–136.

Rogers, C. R. (1961). *On becoming a person*. Boston: Houghton Mifflin.

Roland, A. (1989). *In search of self in India and Japan*. Princeton, NJ: Princeton University Press.

Sacks, O. (1990). *Awakenings*. New York: HarperCollins.

Said, E. (1978). *Orientalism*. New York: Random House.

Sampson, E. E. (1993). Identity politics: Challenges to psychology's understanding. *American Psychologist, 48*(12), 1219–1230.

Sarbin, T. R. (Ed.). (1986). *Narrative psychology: The storied nature of human conduct*. New York: Praeger.

Schon, D. A. (1984). *The reflective practitioner*. New York: Basic Books.

Schwarz, R. A. (1998). From "either-or" to "both-and: Treating dissociative disorders collaboratively." In M. F. Hoyt (Ed.), *The handbook of constructive therapies: Innovative approaches from leading practitioners* (pp. 428–448). San Francisco: Jossey-Bass.

Segall, M. H., Dasen, P. R., Berry, J. W., & Poortinga, Y. H. (1990). *Human behavior in global perspective: An introduction to cross-cultural psychology*. New York: Pergamon.

Shainberg, D. (1983). Teaching therapists how to be with their clients. In J. Welwood (Ed.), *Awakening the heart: East/West approaches to psychotherapy and the healing relationship* (pp. 163–175). Boston, MA: Shambala.

Spence, D. (1984). *Narrative truth and historical truth: Meaning and interpretation in psychoanalysis*. New York: W. W. Norton.

Steenbarger, B. N. (1991). All the world is not a stage: Emerging contextualist themes in counseling and development. *Journal of Counseling and Development, 70*(2), 288–296.

Sue, D. W. (1990). Culture specific strategies in counseling: A conceptual framework. *Professional Psychology, 21*(6), 424–433.

Sue, D. W. (1993). Confronting ourselves: The White and racial/ethnic minority researcher. *The Counseling Psychologist, 21,* 244–249.

Sue, D. W. (1995). Toward a theory of multicultural counseling and therapy. In J. Banks & C. Banks (Eds.), *Handbook of research on multicultural education* (pp. 647–659). New York: Macmillan.

Sue, D. W., Carter, R. T., Casas, J. M., Fouad, N. A., Ivey, A. E., Jensen, M., LaFromboise, T., Manese, J. E., Ponterotto, J. G., & Vazquez-Nutall, E. (1998). *Multicultural counseling competencies: Individual and organizational development*. Thousand Oaks, CA: Sage.

Sue, D. W., Ivey, A., & Pedersen, P. (Eds.). (1996). *A theory of multicultural counseling and therapy*. Pacific Grove, CA: Brooks/Cole.

Sue, D. W., & Sue, D. (1990). *Counseling the culturally different: Theory and practice*. New York: Wiley Interscience.

Taft, J. (1973). *The dynamics of therapy in a controlled relationship*. Gloucester, MA: Peter Smith.

Viney, L. L. (1988). Which data-collection methods are appropriate for a constructive psychology? *International Journal of Personal Construct Psychology, 1,* 191–203.

Vontress, C. E. (1979). Cross-cultural counseling: An existential approach. *Personnel and Guidance Journal, 58,* 117–122.

Vontress, C. E. (1996). A personal retrospective on cross-cultural counseling. *Journal of Multicultural Counseling and Development, 24*(3), 156–166.

Vontress, C. E., Johnson, J. A., & Epp, L. R. (1999). *Cross-cultural counseling: A casebook*. Alexandria, VA: American Counseling Association.

Welwood, J. (1983a). Introduction. In J. Welwood (Ed.), *Awakening the heart: East/West approaches to psychotherapy and the healing relationship* (pp. vii–xiv). Boston, MA: Shambala.

Welwood, J. (1983b). Vulnerability and power in the therapeutic process. In

J. Welwood (Ed.), *Awakening the heart: East/West approaches to psychotherapy and the healing relationship* (pp. 148–162). Boston, MA: Shambala.

White, M., & Epston, D. (1990). *Narrative means to therapeutic ends.* New York: W. W. Norton.

Whitman, W. (1983). *Leaves of Grass.* New York: Bantam.

Wilson, B. (1994a). Working on cultural issues with students: A counseling psychologist's perspective. In G. D. Spindler & L. Spindler (Eds.), *Pathways to cultural awareness: Cultural therapy with teachers and students* (pp. 221–245). Thousand Oaks, CA: Corwin.

Wilson, C. (1994b). When I awoke the world was dreaming. In E. Featherstone (Ed.), *Skin deep: Women writing on color, culture, and identity* (pp. 57–63). Freedom, CA: Crossing Press.

Yalom, I. D. (1980). *Existential psychotherapy.* New York: Basic Books.

Yalom, I. D. (1989). *Love's executioner: And other tales of psychotherapy.* New York: Basic Books.

Yi, K., & Shorter-Gooden, K. (1999). Ethnic identity formation: From stage theory to a constructivist narrative model. *Psychotherapy, 36*(1), 16–26.

Index

About the Author

Stephen Murphy-Shigematsu was born to a Japanese mother and an Irish American father in occupied Japan. He received a doctorate from Harvard University and trained at the National Asian American Psychology Training Center in San Francisco and the Center for Multicultural Training in Psychology in Boston. He was a Fulbright scholar and fellow of the American Psychology Association Minority Fellowship Program. A professor of psychology and ethnic studies at Tokyo University, he is currently a visiting scholar at Stanford University.